T0271452

PRAYING BY HEART

The Lord's Prayer for Everyone

———

STEPHEN COTTRELL

HODDER &
STOUGHTON

First published in Great Britain in 2024 by Hodder & Stoughton
An Hachette UK Company

I

Hardback ISBN 9781399805308
ebook ISBN 9781399805315

Typeset in Sabon MT by Palimpsest Book Production Ltd, Falkirk, Stirlingshire

Printed and bound in Great Britain by Clays Ltd, Elcograf S.p.A.

Hodder & Stoughton policy is to use papers that are natural, renewable
and recyclable products and made from wood grown in sustainable forests.
The logging and manufacturing processes are expected to conform
to the environmental regulations of the country of origin.

Hodder & Stoughton Ltd
Carmelite House
50 Victoria Embankment
London EC4Y 0DZ

The authorised representative in the EEA is Hachette Ireland, 8 Castlecourt
Centre, Castleknock Road, Castleknock, Dublin 15, D15 YF6A, Ireland

www.hodderfaith.com

Sometimes when I'm in such a state of spiritual dryness that I cannot find a single thought in my mind which will bring me close to God, I say an Our Father very slowly indeed.

THÉRÈSE OF LISIEUX[1]

Learning to follow Jesus is simply learning to pray the Lord's Prayer.

TOM WRIGHT[2]

CONTENTS

Our Father in heaven,
hallowed be your name,
your kingdom come,
your will be done,
on earth as in heaven.
Give us today our daily bread.
Forgive us our sins
as we forgive those who sin against us.
Lead us not into temptation
but deliver us from evil.
For the kingdom, the power,
and the glory are yours
now and for ever.
Amen.

Our Father, who art in heaven,
hallowed be thy name;
thy kingdom come;
thy will be done;
on earth as it is in heaven.
Give us this day our daily bread.
And forgive us our trespasses,
as we forgive those who trespass against us.
And lead us not into temptation;
but deliver us from evil.
For thine is the kingdom,
the power, and the glory
for ever and ever.
Amen.

PREFACE

Flowing from the heart of God to the heart of the world, there is no prayer that is better known than the prayer Jesus taught his disciples, what we call the Lord's Prayer.

With brevity, simplicity and splendour, the Lord's Prayer tells us who God is, how we can relate to God, how we can align ourselves with God's purposes for the world, and what we should ask for and hope for. It is an education in desire. When the disciples asked Jesus to teach them to pray, this is what he taught them.[1]

It is a Christian prayer, probably the most famous and well-known prayer in the world. But it is also a prayer shaped by the Jewish tradition that shaped Jesus. It is an incredibly human prayer. A prayer that carries the longings and hopes of everyone. The New Testament scholar John Dominic Crossan says that it comes 'from the heart of Judaism, through the mouth of Christianity to the conscience of the Earth'.[2]

Even today, many people know this prayer by heart.

Knowing something 'by heart' is an interesting English expression. It means we have memorised something. We can recite it without needing the text in front of us.

But could it be more than this? Could it mean that these words and what they convey have moved from the head to the heart? That they have lodged themselves at some deep point in our consciousness, where we are not only able to recall them instantly, but they are shaping how we see and interpret everything else, including how we act?

This is what this book declares. The Lord's Prayer is good for you. It is a pattern for prayer, but also a pattern for life.

Furthermore, when we speak of the things that matter most, we use the language of the heart, not the head. Even though we know, rationally, that the things we learn and the information we retain in our heads – all sorts of things like telephone numbers, PIN numbers, the birthdays of loved ones, the twelve times table and the Lord's Prayer – are lodged in that part of the brain that stores long-term memory, some things, like the Lord's Prayer, are so precious and so important that saying we *know them by heart* feels more appropriate.

Having said that, there are many people – many in the Church – who know the Lord's Prayer by heart, meaning they have memorised it, perhaps from childhood, but it hasn't yet *got* to the heart.

It was a bit different in the early church. Only Christian people knew and said the Lord's Prayer. Learning it by heart – books weren't really available then! – was the culmination of the process that led to baptism. This book, however, is written for those who know it but don't *know* it, as well as for those who don't yet know it at all.

If you already know the Lord's Prayer, I hope this book will encourage you to find out what it means.

If you don't know the Lord's Prayer, I hope this book will encourage you to learn it by heart.

If you are a church leader of any kind, I hope this book will encourage you to teach the Lord's Prayer to others.

Most of all, I hope each one of us will be encouraged to let this prayer of Jesus get into our hearts and shape our lives.

Spoken from the heart of God through the heart of Jesus to the heart of the world, and back to God through the hearts of all those who have learned it by heart, the Lord's Prayer, in under seventy words, is a manifesto for the heart. Learning it, saying it, getting to the heart of it, can change the world.

GETTING STARTED

It is always a great thing to base your prayers on the prayers that were uttered by the very lips of the Lord.

TERESA OF AVILA[1]

The garden of the house where I grew up backed onto a nature reserve.

The entrance was round the corner, and you were only allowed to walk on designated paths. Dogs had to be kept on a lead.

At the entrance, and at various points around 'the woods', as we called them, were fierce signs declaring that trespassing was prohibited and that anyone caught trespassing would be prosecuted. We were to keep to the path.

I cheated, of course. My brothers and I often climbed over the fence from the back garden to play in the woods. The fact that it was forbidden only added to the fun.

There was one memorable occasion when we encountered a park keeper, who chased us home. Fortunately, we were faster than him and, as it turned out, knew that bit of the woods slightly better. We made our escape.

So I grew up knowing that the word 'trespass' meant

'deviation from the prescribed pathway'; going somewhere you shouldn't go.

And, inevitably, like any ordinary, curious and mischievous boy, I took little notice. But I did know what the word meant.

There was virtually no church in my childhood. I was baptised as a baby, and there must have been the odd family occasion – other baptisms, a wedding or two – but those formative childhood years were not in any way shaped by churchgoing or formed by any deep engagement with the Christian faith.

But I did know the Lord's Prayer. This was the 1960s, and even at my secondary school, an unadventurous and largely unchallenging boys' secondary modern, there was an assembly most days and we sang a hymn and said a prayer. I don't really remember how I learned it or from whom. It might have been my parents. It might have been school. But the Lord's Prayer was still sufficiently part of the culture that I'm pretty confident virtually everyone knew it.

The Christian tradition that had shaped our culture for centuries was still known and understood and, to a certain extent, adhered to, even by those who in the 1950s and 1960s were no longer going to church. A steady ebbing away of Christian faith which had started fifty years earlier was gaining pace.

I knew the prayer, but I was puzzled by this word 'trespass'. For me, 'Forgive us our trespasses, as we forgive those who trespass against us' meant 'forgive me when I stray from the path and give me the ability and kindness to forgive others when I see them straying'. But why was it that God seemed to care so much about whether or not I kept off the grass?

Then in the early years of my adolescence I was drawn into the orbit of the Church, and the instinctive belief in God that, though incoherent and unformed, had accompanied me throughout my childhood started to become a narrative and a way of inhabiting life that was now rooted in and shaped by the Christian tradition. I started to discover that it is through Jesus that we come to see and understand God. I also came to understand that Jesus' own thinking and praying were deeply rooted in the revelation of God we find in the Hebrew Scriptures, what Christians call the Old Testament.

Jesus, it turns out, is part of a tradition in which he is the culmination and the turning point. And this was the prayer he taught his disciples. So, it was obviously very important. It could tell me something important about prayer, and because prayer was about communication with God, then it must also have something important to say about God and about God's priorities for the world – the things we should be praying for.

This much I knew, even though the prayer itself, as is the case for many Christians, came and went. What I mean by that is that we know it so well and say it so often, we quickly stop thinking about what the words might mean, still less how they might shape our living as well as our praying.

By now it was the early 1970s, and the Church of England, like much of the worldwide Church, was entering a period of liturgical renewal, where the services of the church and the very language that we used to worship God were being updated and renewed. By the time I actually started going to church, the Book of Common Prayer, which had been the bedrock and the iron rations of Anglican worship for centuries, was no longer used for most of the main services on a Sunday morning. Various alternatives were being experimented with, and even though I had learned the Lord's Prayer with the word 'trespass', that puzzling word was replaced by 'sin'.

Ambiguity was out. Clarity was in. We all knew what sin meant. Or, at least, we thought we did. The prayer was, therefore, now about 'penitence for the things I've done wrong' and not so much about 'the way I've been travelling'. Though, obviously, the two are not separable. But now it seemed there was a sharper edge to the prayer. And still the injunction to forgive others. Though even to my adolescent mind, this felt more problematic than I was expecting. What if the person I had to forgive was not penitent themselves? And what if they carried on doing that which they wilfully knew to be wrong? And were the abused supposed to forgive their abusers?

We will return to these questions when we get to that bit of the prayer, but, for me, the plot thickened when instead of reading the prayer from the service book in church, I happened to read it in the Bible.

First, it seemed there were two versions of the Lord's Prayer: one in Matthew's Gospel, and one in Luke's – and they were not the same. Nor was either of them exactly the same as the prayer we were saying in church, either the new *or* the traditional version.

In Matthew, we were asking God to 'forgive us our debts' (Matthew 6:12), and in Luke, we did ask for our sins to be forgiven, but in response we undertook to 'forgive everyone indebted to us' (Luke 11:4).

Debts, for me, didn't seem quite the same as sins, and sins not really the same as trespasses. They were related, I could see that, but they all seemed to be saying something slightly different.

As I suspect is the case for most of us, the power of repetition won the day. For many years, I worshipped in churches that used the word 'sins'. Consequently, I concluded that this

8

was what the Lord's Prayer meant. But now, many years on, I do think we need to take the concept of debt more seriously in order to understand the prayer – an idea we will return to later. I have also come to have a much greater regard and appreciation for the English liturgical tradition and the powerful impact of that tradition, not just on the lives of individuals, but on a whole culture.

Although it is the case that many people growing up in Britain today don't know the Lord's Prayer at all, in my experience more and more churches are returning to the traditional language of the prayer, for if people do come to church and do know the prayer, it tends to be this version. Therefore, when we say 'sins', they say 'trespasses', and in that moment feel embarrassed and disconnected from the very tradition which they still just about cling on to and came to church to find.

In *Praying by Heart*, I am not trying to make a case for either version of the prayer over the other. Perhaps a good Anglican compromise is to make sure we use both regularly, and exercise real sensitivity towards those who come and are less likely to know the new one. But what I am interested in, and what shapes the whole of this book, is my initial, uninformed but instinctive understanding of what this petition meant: forgive me when I stray from the path and give me the ability and kindness – what the Church calls 'grace' – to forgive others when I see them stray.

This understanding of trespass does not exclude the particularity of sin, nor the moral weight of debt, but it does, straightaway, map out this prayer in a slightly different way. And because this prayer *is* the prayer that Jesus taught his friends (even if our versions are adaptations of one sort or another) all Christian praying (and living!) is about *walking in a way*, following a path, and offering generous understanding and clear direction to those who have not found it, and to those who, for whatever reason, wander from it. As I shall keep on saying in this book, the Lord's Prayer comes from the heart of God to the heart of the world *via* the heart of Jesus and is lived and communicated to the world through *our* hearts. As we learn this prayer by heart and say it each day, we come close to the heart of God and learn to live God's way.

Before the very first followers of Jesus were even called Christians, they were called 'followers of the way'. In John's Gospel, Jesus says, 'I am the way' (John 14:6). And when he calls his disciples, he says, 'Follow me' (Mark 1:17).

The Christian faith is a way of life, not just a list of things to believe in. This prayer, the prayer Jesus gave us, is a pattern for our living as well as our praying. It is the heart of prayer.

The Lord's Prayer, says Tom Wright, 'is a lens through which to see Jesus . . . and discover what he is about'.[2] In giving us this prayer, Jesus is giving us his very self, his heart. 'It is a prayer to be lived,' says Robert Warren.[3]

The Lord's Prayer is, therefore, the mountain peak of prayer whose summit we may never quite reach, its expectations of how we live being so very high. But it is also the deep well that we can easily draw from every day, finding here the sustenance and consolation that we need. It will teach us the way by teaching us what we need, to whom we must give thanks and to whom we must give account.

How to get the best out of this book

The great Anglican priest and theologian Austin Farrer described the Lord's Prayer as 'three hearty wishes and three humble requests'.[4] Therefore, after we have declared our belonging to each other and our intimacy with God by uttering the words 'Our Father', there are three further declarations about the holiness of God and of God's name; a crying out for God's kingdom to be established; and an expression of confident hope and heartfelt intent that God's will may be done.

These three hearty wishes are, therefore, also three hearty praises. We praise God for who God is and for God's will and purposes to be known *on earth as in heaven*.

This phrase – on earth as in heaven – is like a hinge between the first and second parts of the prayer. We move from addressing God as God is, to addressing our needs in the world, what Farrer calls 'three humble requests': give us our daily bread; forgive us and help us to be forgiving; deliver us from evil and lead us not into temptation.

In order to get inside and understand the Lord's Prayer I have structured the book around these praises and requests.

Part 1 focuses on the crucially important opening phrase itself: Our Father. Part 2 explores the meaning of the three hearty wishes; Part 3, the three humble requests. Part 4 is that bit of the prayer that isn't found in Scripture, 'For thine is the kingdom, the power and the glory, for ever and ever. Amen' because it is part of the prayer we say and will help us draw everything together.

In this way we will go through the Lord's Prayer word by word, line by line and part by part discovering what it means for our praying and our living.

It is the sort of book you can sit down and read all at once, but I recommend that the best way of reading it is with others. As you are about to discover, the very first word of the prayer shapes everything that follows. So just as Jesus teaches us that we belong to God and to each other and can only find the fulfilment we long for in community with God and in community with others, so all prayer – even when we're on our own – is a communal activity. We join our prayer with the prayer of the whole Church, with Christian people everywhere, with the song of the angels in heaven, and, most astonishing of all, with the prayer of Jesus himself. When we cry 'Father' (the second word of the Lord's Prayer), it is the Holy Spirit praying in us, says Paul (see Romans 8:15–16).

Therefore, reading and reflecting on this book with others may be the best way to read it. In which case, I suggest that you read the book as part of a group or a study course.

At the back of the book, you will find a suggested pattern for this way of reading and studying the book and questions that you can address.

Part One

OUR FATHER IN HEAVEN

Each time we say 'Our Father' we state that the word
Father *cannot stand on its own, apart from* Our.
POPE FRANCIS[1]

The first two words of the Lord's Prayer are a revolution in the way we think about God and the way we think about ourselves.

To call God 'Father' in the same way Jesus called God 'Father' is to enter into a relationship with God where we have access to God, understanding of God, and where we find ourselves profoundly loved. We share God's fatherhood with Jesus. Jesus shares it with us.

And to begin with the word 'Our' is a declaration that everyone else with whom we say this prayer is sister and brother.

However, in the Greek New Testament where we first find this prayer written down, the word 'Father' comes first, the literal translation of the Greek being 'Father of us', which we have then rendered in English 'Our Father'.

This arrangement of the words, 'Father' coming first, would have been the same in the Aramaic that Jesus spoke and therefore the actual order of the words that Jesus gave his disciples.

To think about God as our loving Father and understand what this word means and how we can use it and understand it today is the place to begin.

And 'if we do not begin our prayer with this word, spoken, not with our lips, but with our hearts – not the Almighty God, not a cosmic God, but a Father', says Pope Francis, 'we cannot pray as Christians.'[2]

2.

FATHER – THE INTIMACY AND AFFIRMATION OF LOVE

I was very blessed to be born and brought up in a loving, generous and affirming family. This has shaped how I think and feel about many things, not least myself and my relationships with others. But I've come to know that it is not like this for everyone.

While I have never doubted I was loved, some people never get to experience love at all. They just don't really know what love is. The relationships that are meant to nurture and sustain them only let them down. Worse than that, they leave them insecure and anxious about whether they can ever be lovable.

Worst of all, for some people, those to whom they look for the security and affirmation they need neglect and abuse them.

But this wasn't my story. I experienced the affirmation of love, and I know the difference it makes. It has led me to understand that the greatest gift one human being can give to another is the gift of affirmation, the gift of knowing that another person – and even better, if it is the person who bore you and brought you into the world – is on your side and believes in you, and that the love they have for you is without condition.

In other words, they don't love you because of all the things you've achieved, nor for how you look, or for your abilities, but *just because you are*. It is your being, your very self, which is the source of their delight. And when you receive such unconditional love, you find that you are able to love others in the same way. This love is an ever-replenishing source of goodness and affirmation. As I say, it is quite simply the greatest gift that one human being can give to another.

Not only did I receive and experience this love in my home and from my parents, and with my brothers and sister, but also at crucial points in my life from other people who believed in me. After a bit of a rocky education, where I ended up with only a handful of O-levels, I found myself enrolled in a new sixth form, and the teachers there believed in me. They saw something in me. They nurtured the gifts that had hitherto lain dormant. They helped me become myself. Their affirmation saved me. They were giving me something of the affirmation that a loving parent and a loving God can give.

I've always liked writing. Throughout my life it has been a compulsive joy. Now that I have a role within the Church of England that carries large responsibilities, people often say to me, 'How do you find time to write?' I don't really know how to answer the question. It feels a little bit like asking, 'How do you find time to breathe?' Writing for me is so woven into the way I live and make sense of life that I simply can't imagine *not* finding the time, though even that expression seems to be the wrong one. I don't *find* time to write. The writing finds me. For as long as I can remember, and even when I was a very small boy, I wrote. And I wrote as many books, and just as much, before I was fortunate enough to have books published as I have done since.

But it might have been different. In the first school I went to, nobody took much notice of my writing. It wasn't a school with very high expectations. Most people left for the workplace at fifteen. I loved it when the teachers invited us to write a story, and because whenever I put pen to paper stuff just poured out, the teachers left me to get on with it, although they did hand back my work covered with red ink, showing how little I knew about spelling and grammar, though this was surely their responsibility!

But once I started writing, I just had to get everything out. And at that point I didn't know much about grammar. My spelling *was* awful. And it was as much my fault as the teachers', because I wasn't then the sort of boy who was much interested in learning that sort of thing. What was driving me was the need to tell the story. What I was discovering was the profound mystery of communication; that we human beings need to say things and to write things in order to know them and understand them. Surely this is why Jesus gave us a prayer!

Then, in a different educational environment, I was taught English by Mrs Bareham. To this day, I can remember the first time she handed back a piece of work I had written – a very personal reflection on a poem. I hadn't really followed the instructions for the task, nor had my spelling or grammar improved one iota, but she had seen something in the writing, and in me. She encouraged and affirmed me, and told me that I had the fiercely glowing embers of a gift that needed to be fanned into fire. It was this affirmation, and the huge encouragement it gave me, which compelled me to learn how to spell and to find out where to put the commas. It not only kept me writing, but it enabled the writing to take better shape with greater clarity.

I am blessed: by parents who loved me without condition;

by teachers who saw something in me just when it was needed; and throughout my life by the friendships and affirmation of many others who have upheld me.

At the same time, I can remember friends at school who didn't have the support I had; and in my pastoral ministry as a priest and a bishop, I have seen the traumatising damage of neglect and abuse, and the horror and insecurity it can breed.

Jesus the beloved son

Jesus was born into a loving family. We know very little about his childhood, but we see in Mary, his mother, a model of steadfast commitment and devotion. Only a mother who loved without condition or reserve could stand at the foot of the cross as she did. And Joseph, her husband, stood by her when she was pregnant, and committed himself to her and her unborn son, when it would have been so easy for him to walk away.

And even though we know very little about Jesus' childhood, we know it had its all too ordinary moments, as when Jesus got separated from his family on the return from Jerusalem and his parents couldn't find him. Hurrying back to Jerusalem in their anxiety, they discovered him in the temple, teaching the teachers. 'Did you not know that I must be in my Father's house?' said Jesus (Luke 2:49).

Here is the abiding source of affirmation for Jesus: not just the love of an earthly family, but the affirmation of a very loving God.

At his baptism the heavens are opened, and the Spirit of God descends like a dove, and a voice cries out, 'This is my

Son, the Beloved, with whom I am well pleased' (Matthew 3:17).

It is the voice of God, the voice of affirmation and of unconditional love. The voice of delight.

In fact, whereas in Matthew's Gospel, quoted above, God speaks about Jesus in the third person, announcing something to all the crowd as well as to Jesus, in Mark's Gospel the same story has an even more personal and intimate character to it: God speaks to Jesus directly, saying, '*You* are my Son, the Beloved' (Mark 1:11, my italics).

Some biblical scholars reflect that the whole of Jesus' ministry, everything that proceeds from his baptism, is undertaken in the strength and resolve that comes from this affirmation.

We, on the other hand, might expect God to say something a little more interesting and profound. After all, the heavens don't open that often, and God rarely speaks so directly. But, actually, is there anything more profound that God could say? Either to Jesus, or to us? In the midst of the horrors and confusions of the world, and with all our shortcomings, and in the many ways we let ourselves and each other down, and in our failure to love one another, God believes in us – God hopes for us. Which is why, in Matthew's slightly less intimate version of the story, it is so lovely that although God is speaking *about Jesus*, he is actually speaking *directly to us*.

Jesus already knows he is beloved of God. Though even for him, in this moment of baptism, of solidarity with us in our sinfulness, this affirmation from God must have been of huge significance and a source of great strength.

And you can never get too much affirmation. Nor, like love, does the supply ever run dry, since it is ever replenishing.

In the act of giving affirmation to others, we also receive it. In fact, we can see here, in the affirmation of God the Father to God the Son, a window into the ever-replenishing reciprocity of love, which is the very life of God, whom we Christians understand to be a community of persons, Father, Son and Holy Spirit.

But what is also interesting is what God is saying to us about God's great love for Jesus. Three things are of critical importance:

1. God tells us that Jesus is God's Son.
2. God tells us that Jesus is God's beloved.
3. God tells us that Jesus is the one in whom God is pleased.

The promise of the Christian faith, and therefore the promise to those who say this prayer, is that these three things that God says to Jesus, God also says to us. That whatever has gone wrong in our lives, and wherever life has let us down, we can, through Jesus, come into a relationship with God where we find ourselves to be the children of God; where we find ourselves to be the beloved of God; and where we come to know that God is on our side, that God believes in us, and that we receive the affirmation of God's love.

This is good news for everyone, but it is especially good for those who have been hurt and excluded by the travails and privations of life, and those who have been let down by those who should have loved them.

Receiving this good news isn't always easy. Abuse and neglect have a tight grip and constrict the heart. Letting love in may have to happen slowly. Nevertheless, it remains true: God is there for us, no matter what else has laid siege to our hearts.

And because God calls Jesus his Son, this means that God is a parent, and loves us as the very best parent a parent could be. And we can know that this parent, the one who is God, is the one who made us, and is the source of everything, the one whose very name is Love.

Jesus called God 'Father'

The first word we are looking at in our exploration of the Lord's Prayer is the word Jesus used when he spoke to God and when he talked about God to others. It is beautiful, surprising and very challenging.

Although in the Old Testament there are a few places where God is referred to as a 'Father' ('You are my Father, my God, and the Rock of my salvation' says Psalm 89:26), in the liturgy of the synagogue, and the everyday prayers that Jesus knew so well, this was not how God was addressed. Indeed, the most ancient traditions of Judaism would have told him that the name of God is something we cannot know or utter.

Going right back to Moses at the burning bush, another occasion when God speaks directly, Moses asks God to tell him his name. But God doesn't quite answer, replying, enigmatically, 'I am who I am' (Exodus 3:14). After this, the Hebrew letters that made up the first of each of these words became a kind of substitute for the 'unknowable' name of God.

You will see this in some English translations of the Bible, where the letters themselves – YHWH – are turned into a word, *Yahweh*. Generally, these letters are simply translated as 'the Lord'. But the point is that we do not know and cannot know the name of God, just as in the same way we cannot see God. That's why when Moses hides in a cleft in the rock as God passes by, God covers Moses so that he does not see God's face, but only God's back. Even then, the dazzling glory of God is reflected on Moses' face. This so terrifies the people that Moses covers his face with a veil.

Having said that, although the word 'Father' may not have been used very much, the *idea* of God's fatherhood of Israel was central to Israel's understanding of itself. In other words, as one of my predecessors put it, 'the springs of this teaching are to be found in the Old Testament'.[1] Psalm 103 says that God's compassion for his children is like that of a father. The prophet Hosea describes Israel as a child (Hosea 11:1). And the prophet Isaiah says, 'You, O LORD, are our father; our Redeemer from of old is your name' (Isaiah 63:16).

So when Moses stood before Pharaoh and said, 'Thus says the LORD [YHWH – the holy unnameable name of God]: Israel is my firstborn son' (Exodus 4:22), he was actually referencing the fatherhood of God.

Therefore, these Hebrew slaves were children of God.

Jesus also understood his mission as one of liberation, releasing every person in the world to be a child of God.

He understood his vocation to be that of Israel. To set people free. To be the light of the world.

Therefore, it is beautiful and astonishing that Jesus, clearly drawing on some of the strands of the Jewish tradition in which he has been formed, but also transcending it, pulls it all together by openly calling God 'Father'.

In fact, the word we think Jesus often used for 'Father' is the Aramaic word *Abba*. The best translation of this in English is probably 'Dad' or even 'Daddy'. It is the word a child uses to speak to their loving father in the beautiful simplicity of trusting and accepting familiarity.

Only one example of this remains in the Gospels. Mostly, the Aramaic Jesus spoke is translated into the Greek in which the New Testament is written. But in Mark's Gospel, on the night before he dies, and in agony in Gethsemane, Jesus says, 'Abba, Father, for you all things are possible; remove this cup from me; yet, not what I want, but what you want' (Mark 14:36). This, as we shall come to see in a later chapter, leads us into other important truths about the prayer Jesus gave us.

In John's Gospel, where Jesus consistently speaks of God as 'the Father', another word, *pater* or *patros,* is used. John writes that Jesus is the one who is 'close to the Father's heart' (John 1:18). And resting close to the Father's heart, Jesus can speak *to* God, and speak *of* God, with beautiful familiarity and trust.

There are lots of other examples. 'If you know me, you will know my Father also,' says Jesus (John 14:7). 'If you ask anything of the Father in my name, he will give it to you' (John 16:23).

The point, however, is consistent and plain: Jesus addresses God as Father. He encourages us to do the same. And by referring to God as *the* Father, Jesus emphasises that God is not just *a* father among other fathers, as God is not just *a* God among other gods, *but the God and Father of all of us.*

When the disciples ask him to teach them to pray, he begins with this word, the word that *he* uses to address God: 'Father' (Luke 11:2).

In Matthew's Gospel, the Lord's Prayer is introduced with the words, 'Pray then in this way: 'Our Father' (Matthew 6:9).

God the strength and goodness of fatherhood
and the love and wisdom of motherhood

Of course, none of this means that God is male. God, who is the source and origin of everything that is, and whose being – the being upon which the whole creation is contingent – is outside of the space and time in which we live and exist, is neither male nor female.

We are created in the image of this God, and we are created in diversity. The good God whose good, though fallen, creation is made in good and flourishing diversity; not just the diversity of male and female, but everything else we are learning about human identity, and what is often a spectrum of identities. Therefore, within the life of God, there is maleness and femaleness and everything else besides. But God, in God's very being, is outside this and beyond this.

God became human in the particular specificity of Jesus, whose gender was male, and who in turn uses the male language of 'Father' to describe his and our relationship with God. But God is not male.

Furthermore, as Christians, we cannot talk of God without talking of the God who is Father, Son and Holy Spirit, a community of persons. This community further emphasises the beauty of the diversity we see in God and through which God has made the universe. The creation, with all its astonishing variety (of which we are a part), is itself a reflection of the God in whose image we have been made.

So, we call God 'Father' in continuity with the tradition that comes from Jesus himself. But we also know that God is 'Mother', and there is a long tradition of this going back to certain passages of Scripture. For example, Jesus speaks of how he longs to gather God's people together, 'as a hen gathers her brood under her wings' (Matthew 23:37). And in the book of Proverbs, wisdom is described with feminine pronouns.

A famous prayer of St Anselm, written in the eleventh century and now part of the Church of England's liturgy, begins: 'Jesus, like a mother you gather your people to you; you are gentle with us as a mother with her children.'[2]

Mother Julian of Norwich, an anchoress writing in the fourteenth century, says that it is in the nature of God to set good against evil, and that, therefore, Christ himself, who overcame evil with good, 'is our true Mother'.[3]

'God is as really our mother as he is our Father,' she writes. 'God,' she says, 'is the strength and goodness of fatherhood . . . the wisdom of motherhood . . . and the light and grace of blessed love.'[4]

A little later on she says that the word 'mother' is 'so fine and lovely . . . so sweet and so much its own that it cannot be used of any but Jesus'.[5]

It is quite astonishing for some Christians to read this today. It was very *very* astonishing in the fourteenth century. But it helpfully shows us that the fatherhood of God also includes the motherhood of God. For Julian all this flowed from the words she heard God say to her: 'It is I whom you love.'[6] It was the revelation of God's love that led her to see God as Mother and Father.

In our own day, as we have slowly come to terms with the beautiful diversity and complexity of human identity, so we have also been led to a deeper understanding of what Paul was pointing us towards when he said that in Christ there is no longer male and female, but a new humanity (Galatians 3:26–28).

Consequently, this has enabled us to benefit from thinking

about God as Mother as well as Father, even if it hasn't – and maybe even shouldn't – change the time-honoured ways in which we pray most of the time. But we must be keenly aware that for those who have suffered abuse from their earthly father, or suffered clerical abuse in the Church from clergy – some of whom may have wished to be addressed as 'Father' – it is very hard, in fact virtually impossible, to say that name to God. It has been entirely overtaken by their negative and oppressive experiences.

Furthermore, many women and girls and LGBTQI+ people have suffered from or been marginalised and excluded by the overly patriarchal ways in which society has been ordered in the past – behaviour that sadly still continues in our day. We see this in the inequalities women and girls still experience, and the prejudice and disdain that many LGBTQI+ people still have to deal with.

But I'm not saying we should get rid of the word 'Father'. Far from it. We need to help people see that whereas earthly fathers have let them down, God, who is the 'loving unconditionally Father' of our Lord Jesus Christ, is there to heal and redeem.

This may take time, however, so meanwhile we need to be aware that the word can be problematic for some people. We, therefore, need to be sensitive in the way we help people enter into this part of the Christian tradition.

Stephen Cherry, in his book on the Lord's Prayer, *Thy Will Be Done*, speaks of God as 'the motherly father'.[7] This is a delightful way of seeking to capture in prayer the type of God that we speak about when we call God 'Father'. He is not proposing, and neither am I, that there should be any change to the Lord's Prayer. But I hope that most sensitive pastors and priests will want to be aware of how loaded and troublesome some words can be for some people through absolutely no fault of their own.

But let me be clear: I want people to come to know God as their Father.

I want them to know that God is the Father who will never let them down.

I want them to know that God loves them and delights in them just because they are.

I also want them to know that God is a Mother to them. And so much else besides.

For some people, I know, it will take a little while to help them get there, which is why sometimes we won't overuse the word 'Father' in our prayers, opting to use phrases like 'Loving God' when we begin to pray.

But Jesus *did* use the word 'Father'. He knew the security and affirmation of a loving home. He knew God to be his loving Father. He had such intimacy with God that it was a delight for him to find time to be with the Father, and in those times, he used the word a small child uses, because he rested secure in the knowledge of his Father's love. He rested in the heart of God. There are many examples of this in the Gospels. Jesus gets away from the clamour and demands of the crowds, and even from the disciples themselves, so he can spend time with the Father. It is the bedrock and the wellspring of his ministry.

This is the first thing the Lord's Prayer teaches us. It teaches us the nature of our relationship with God. It teaches us that God is available to us. It teaches us that God loves us unconditionally. It shows us that the heart of prayer is simply to rest in the presence of God and to know God's love for us in Jesus Christ; that we, too, are God's beloved.

It shows us that we have access to God.

We, too, the beloved of God

I have a busy life. Just about every minute of my day is accounted for – often for months or even years in advance. In fact, since I took on my responsibilities as the ninety-eighth Archbishop of York, I have had a little team of people whose chief work is to look after and manage my diary. It's not that people can't get to see me, but they do have to make an appointment. There is a process they have to go through. I am available, but my availability is carefully managed.

There is, however, one exception.

If my kids phone, even though they are now all grown up and have fled the nest, I pick up.

If I'm in a meeting, I send a quick message saying that when the meeting is over, I'll phone back.

They don't have to make an appointment. They don't go through my diary secretary. They don't have to negotiate my entirely lovely, but necessarily strict, PA.

I am their dad, and they are my children, and we have direct access to each other. Whatever the day and whatever the time. There is no greater priority in my life than their well-being. I love them absolutely, wholeheartedly, and without condition. They still (sometimes) drive me round the bend, but there is absolutely nothing they can do that will stop me loving them. It is, quite simply, impossible.

Even if I imagine them committing the most heinous crime, depraving themselves, crushing my spirit and destroying what little reputation I might have, I still cannot even begin to imagine that I would be capable of not loving them. And by love, I mean believing in them, and always and for ever wanting what is good for them and delighting just to know they are.

Yes, in such unthinkably awful circumstances, the most likely expression of my love would be tears; endless, unremitting tears. But they would be the tears of a love that cannot let go, that is simply unable to stop.

This is how God loves us. This is why Paul says that nothing can separate us from the love of God.[8] God delights in us and believes in us in the same way a parent delights and believes in their children.

It is the first thing the Lord's Prayer teaches us. It is captured in a single word. It is the word Jesus himself used and the one he encourages us to use. We must use it sensitively. We must understand that it can be difficult for some people. But we do not let go of it, because it tells us that we are in a relationship with God. And like the very best relationships between a parent and a child – in fact, how those relationships are meant to be – there is nothing about it which is transactional. It is not *if you behave in the way I expect you to, I will love you*, so that love is turned into a reward, and therefore not really love at all. It is *I love you because you are*. It is I have loved you from the very first moment of your being. Even before your parents knew that you were, I loved you. And even if you turn your back on me, and even if you fail to be the person you are meant to be, and waste your life and end up doing horrid, horrid things, I will go on loving you.

And because the love God offers is not a reward, God is not looking for anything in return. However, the tiniest sign or acknowledgement that we feel this love too, that we return this love, and that we might actually love God, will be the greatest, greatest joy – the very joy in heaven that Jesus speaks about when one sinner (i.e., one of us!) repents.[9]

We Christians believe that God is a kind and glorious,

giving and receiving God, where between Father, Son and Holy Spirit there is an ever-replenishing and affirming mutuality of love.

Moreover, the invitation of the Christian faith is to be included in this relationship. The whole purpose of the Christian faith is that God comes to us in Jesus, so that we may know that we are the beloved too, that we are the ones in whom God is pleased, and for whom God's heart longs.

I suppose we cannot really say the Lord's Prayer until we know that this is what we are saying, and that this is the promise we are holding on to.

But when we say it, when we name God 'Father', however hesitantly, and maybe with much foreboding, the heavens open and God comes to us, and is astonishingly pleased with us. And we know ourselves, with all our shortcomings and failings, and with the many ways we need to amend our lives, to be the beloved of God, the little children we need to become in order to be great in the kingdom of heaven.[10]

3.

OUR – THE BEAUTIFUL
CHALLENGE OF BELONGING

I recently visited Rome for the first time. I was the guest of
the Anglican Centre, which is a kind of Anglican outpost
and embassy in the eternal city, and a centre for ecumenical
dialogue and hospitality.

It was a fabulous visit.

The main purpose was a public conversation with Cardinal
Tagle, discussing how disunity between Christians damages
our witness. After all, on the night before he died, Jesus
prayed that the Church would be one so that the world would
believe (John 17:20–21). At that point, 'the Church' was just
the eleven disciples gathered round Jesus in the upper room
(Judas had already gone out to betray him), but even then,
Jesus could see how easy it was for people to disagree with
one another, how depressing the inevitable conflict and division would be, and how damaging its impact to the central
purposes of the gospel. The disciples then, as now, often
argued with one another about who was the most important.

Sadly, Jesus was right. He usually is. His plea to his disciples fell on deaf ears. The history of the Church which bears
his name is a history of astonishing service, an amazing
expansion into all the cultures and nations of the world, but

also a bloody story of conflict, oppression, human failure and division.

In our own day, although there have been real steps forward in dialogue between what is now a tapestry of different Christian denominations, most of us have simply got used to the idea that there are different churches and that they largely run on parallel lines.

Not only is this a scandal to God, but it is also probably one of the major reasons that those who do not yet know Christ are put off the message of the gospel. After all, if followers of Jesus can't even be reconciled to each other, why should they take seriously our claim to have a message of reconciliation for the whole world?

On that same night before he died, when Jesus prayed that the Church would be one, he also gave his disciples the meal that would be the way they remembered him. Breaking bread, pouring wine, he showed them how to make a perpetual remembrance of his dying and rising, and how this would bring them together into a new humanity. But in the Church today, we can't even come together to share this bread and wine. What was *one* communion appears to be *several*.

There is hope. All mainstream Christian denominations acknowledge each other's baptism, and this is something we can and must build on. But what is still most shocking is the way we continue to take our disunity for granted. We have become habituated to it. We aren't scandalised. We think it's normal.

With all this in my mind as I travelled to Rome, I knew that part of my visit would be an audience with Pope Francis.

I was excited and nervous.

With my wife and a few colleagues, I arrived at the Vatican

with a little trepidation. I wasn't sure what to expect. Would we be ushered in, exchange a few pleasantries and then be on our way? Or might it be something more?

Well, it was.

We did indeed exchange pleasantries. But then the Pope ushered us into the adjacent parlour, where we sat and talked.

It wasn't a long conversation, but for about twenty minutes we talked together about the scandal of our disunity, about the bond of a common baptism, and about the need, as Pope Francis put it, 'to walk together, to work together, and to pray together'.

In other words, perhaps we need to stop seeing unity as something to be achieved by intellectual agreement; that it isn't so much about solving the complicated questions of the past, which were the cause of our breaking away from each other, and all the other complex, political demonstrations of power that have been, and probably still are, tightly woven into our discussions, disagreements and reasons for splitting. It is about seeing that we are *already one in Jesus Christ*, and that because of our baptism we already belong to each other. The task, therefore, may not be to unravel the twisted knots of the unity we don't have, but to reveal the unity we do have. And build on it. And do something new. Then the other issues would start to unravel of their own accord. We would *discover* unity. Not achieve it. And maybe the best way to begin is to do things together: to walk together, work together, and pray together.

Then we did just that. We prayed. And the Pope led us in the Lord's Prayer, the prayer that is the heart of all prayer, the prayer that belongs to all Christians, the prayer that Jesus taught us.

We were an international little gathering in that room, so we each said the prayer in our mother tongue. Yet, at the same time, we all knew we were saying the same thing: the same words to the same God that we had learned from the same God.

What was binding us together in that moment was our common faith in Jesus Christ, and our desire to follow him and learn from him. He was the one who had taught us to pray this way. Words from the heart of God to our hearts.

It was in that moment that the power of the opening word of the Lord's Prayer in English really struck me.

Not *my* God or *your* God.

Not *my* Father or *your* Father.

Ours.

Just saying this prayer was a declaration of the unity we already had. Now we needed to work to make it visible. It meant, whether I liked it or not, that everyone else who said this prayer *was* my sister or my brother. We belonged to each other.

Our belonging in Christ

'Whoever does the will of my Father in heaven is my brother and sister and mother,' says Jesus (Matthew 12:50). And as if to really emphasise the point, it is on Easter Day itself that Jesus says to Mary Magdalen that he is 'ascending to my Father and your Father, to my God and your God' (John 20:17). *The* Father has now really become *our* Father.

To say the Lord's Prayer is to articulate the will and purposes of God. It binds us to each other in a community whose membership we are not able to control or police, because it comes from our belonging to God through Jesus. We are all children of the same heavenly Father.

Jesus is the one who counts us in. We cannot therefore ever have the power to declare people out.

And, of course, if we belong to each other, then we have a responsibility to each other. Whatever someone's nationality or denomination or language or ethnicity or culture or sexuality, everyone who says this prayer is part of the household of God, the very household and community of faith that Jesus has made possible through his death and resurrection, breaking down those barriers of separation that we so love to erect. Therefore, to say this prayer, just the opening two words, is to say something astonishing and powerful about who we are in relationship to each other across the world, and who we are in relationship to God.

Jesus taught us to love our neighbour, but in saying this prayer, the challenge of living this out is brought into an even tighter focus: the person who is my neighbour who says this prayer with me, *is* a member of my family, my household. They *are* my brother and sister.

As ever, Pope Francis himself has expressed this with beautiful simplicity. 'I am not an only child,' he writes, 'none of us is.'[1]

Moreover, the fact that it is *our* God, not *my* God, runs through the whole prayer.

So, imagine for a moment that the prayer was not written this way. Imagine it was the first-person singular, 'My Father', not the first-person plural, 'Our'. It wouldn't just change the prayer; it would destroy it.

Give me *my* daily bread. Forgive me *my* sins. This is a narrow, nasty, selfish way of praying. It is all about me and what I want.

The prayer only works because it is plural. And because it is 'ours' it is broad, challenging and beautiful.

Once again, we discover that what is best for us is found in community with others; that we cannot be ourselves on our own. Our well-being is tied up with the well-being of our neighbour.

It is our isolation from one another, and from God, which is the problem and the besetting sin of all humanity. We see this in those old, old stories at the beginning of the book of Genesis, where we read about how sin came into the world. Adam and Eve, who are made for community with each other and for community with God, turn on each other, blame each other and even try to hide from God. Cain slays his brother Abel.

A whole sorry history of separation and failure unfolds.

Empires rise and fall.

Barriers of separation grow.

Walls get higher. Trenches are dug deeper.

All because we do not love each other; do not think we belong to each other; fail to take responsibility for each other, and indulge the fantasy that it is possible to hide from God. We do this so effectively today that we've even managed to convince ourselves that God doesn't exist.

But God is not to be messed with. And because God is the God who is love, and is the Father, Son and Holy Spirit God, and because all love wants is to expand the horizons of love so that the reciprocity of giving and receiving the love that is within God might be shared with the whole creation, God steps into the world. God in Jesus is reconciling the world, showing us what love looks like, breaking down barriers and rolling stones away.

God is saving us from ourselves.

God is teaching us how to pray, which is about learning how to live our lives in communion with God and in communion with each other. By giving us this particular prayer, and by its repetition so that it dwells deeply within us, God is teaching us how to live.

This is the big picture of this little book: the Lord's Prayer is a pattern for life, not only a pattern for prayer. Right praying, we discover, shapes right living. We learn this prayer by heart and our hearts are changed. We read the prayer, but also the prayer reads us.

We are called not just to say 'Our Father' but to live as good neighbours and sisters and brothers within the whole household of the human family; to know that, in Jesus, we have access to God, as a child with its father or mother and with the same intimacy of love. We are given the opportunity of living life God's way.

Which is why I want to say two more things about the Lord's Prayer before we move into the main body of the prayer itself.

First, be careful with this prayer.

All our prayer books and service sheets should carry a health warning. 'Be warned!' they should say. 'This prayer will change you. It will change the way you think about yourself. It will change the way you think about others. It will change the way you think about God.'

Second, don't say this prayer if you are not prepared to be changed; and particularly, don't say this prayer if you are not prepared to be the answer to the prayer you offer.

What I mean by this is that because prayer is not just words, but communication and relationship with God, then to say, 'Your will be done. . .', 'Give us our daily bread . . .', 'Help us to forgive others . . .' is not the wistful dreaming of an impossible ideal we can't possibly live up to and probably won't ever attempt. It is *a declaration of intent.*

This is how we intend to live our lives. We intend to seek God's will. We want to work for a world where all are fed. We want forgiveness and reconciliation to be the hallmarks of our lives and of our public life and be the way we deal with each other, whether it is our neighbour across the street or the nations of the world.

This is what I mean by being an answer to our own prayers. If we say in our prayers that we want the hungry to be fed, then we need to ask ourselves what we are doing to feed the hungry.

If we pray, 'God's will be done on earth as in heaven,' then we need to ask ourselves how our lives conform to and demonstrate the will of God as we see it in Jesus Christ.

And at this point, you may want to stop reading the book, because this is very hard indeed.

Suddenly, the prayer that seemed so simple and straightforward becomes the hardest challenge you will ever face.

Indeed, we start to wonder: 'Can I ever say this prayer and truly mean it?'

But please don't stop reading.

It is hard. It is challenging. But the prayer itself, not least these two opening words, also carries the hope that will see us through without ever letting us off the hook.

In this prayer, as should be the case with all Christian prayer, we come to God only too aware of our shortcomings, misgivings, failures and pride. After all, this is the prayer that says, 'Forgive us our sins . . . forgive us our trespasses.'

'For I have the desire to do what is good, but I cannot carry it out,' says Paul. 'I do not do the good I want to do, but the evil I do not want to do – this I keep on doing' (Romans 7:18b–19, NIV).

This is a predicament familiar to all of us. We are not the

people we want to be, let alone the people God wants us to be.

Nevertheless, in all his letters, Paul's great watchword is 'persevere'. He knows his need of God. So do we.

Therefore, we persevere.

We persevere, knowing that the God who loves us is the God of mercy and justice; the God who holds before us the high ideal of a Christ-like life is the God who knows that we stumble and fall.

We keep saying this prayer, because by the Holy Spirit praying within us (more on this later), these words change us, and our lives begin to demonstrate the things we learn. God will truly be our loving Father. We are God's children.

As we learn this, and by the patient, persevering repetition of this prayer, we come closer to Christ and, through Christ, closer to the Father's heart. This is good news for our lives and good news for the world.

It also means we come closer to each other. The unity that we already have in Christ is revealed. This will be very good for the Church, but much more importantly, as Jesus prayed, it will bring belief and hope and peace to the world; a world still so angrily divided, still so suspicious of others, still crying out for all the good things this prayer promises.

Living and serving at one of the most anguished and turbulent times for the Christian church in Europe, Hugh Latimer was a Church of England martyr of the Reformation period. He was Bishop of Worcester for a short time, and was a brilliant and popular advocate for the reformed faith and a lively and provocative preacher. But when Mary Tudor came to the throne in 1553, Latimer was sent to the Tower of London. In the following year, together with Ridley, he was burnt as a heretic in Oxford.

Many of his sermons and writings survive. They are inspired reading, particularly his spiritual writings, and for me particularly his preaching about the Lord's Prayer. He too homed in on the word 'our'.

I finish this chapter with his beautiful and challenging words:

He saith not 'my' but 'our' . . . This word 'our' teacheth us to consider that the Father of heaven is a common Father; as well my neighbour's Father as mine; as well the poor man's Father as the rich: so that he is not a peculiar Father, but a Father to the whole church and congregation, to all the faithful. Be they never so poor, so vile, so foul and despised, yet he is their Father as well as mine: and therefore I should not despise them, but consider that God is their Father as well as mine . . . When I pray, I pray not for myself alone, but for all the rest: again, when they pray, they pray, not for themselves only, but for me: for Christ hath so framed this prayer, that I must . . . include my neighbour in it. Therefore, all those which pray this prayer, they pray as well for me, as for themselves, which is a great comfort to every faithful heart, when he considereth that all the church prayeth for him.[2]

Part Two

THREE HEARTY PRAISES

Of course, God can run the universe without our help, but he has chosen not to, and though many things are God's will – peace and justice for starters – they will not happen unless and until we actively seek and work for them.

MICHAEL MAYNE[1]

The Roman Catholic theologian John Dominic Crossan, writing about the revolutionary message of the Lord's Prayer, also invites us to pay attention to how 'well crafted, carefully organised and poetically structured'[2] the prayer is. He particularly pays attention to the order of the words in the Greek language in which we first find the prayer written down.

Although we say 'Our Father' because that works in English, the actual order of the words is much more like 'Father of us'. Then there are the first three petitions which Crossan helpfully sets out in English in a way that helps us appreciate and understand the flow and poetry of the Greek:

Be hallowed	the	name of you
Be come	the	kingdom of you
Be done	the	will of you[3]

In each case the verb comes first – *be hallowed*, *be come*, *be done*. In fact, they sound like commands.

But to whom are they directed?

Well, to God; this is, after all, a prayer.

But also to us.

As we say this prayer we are invited into a collaborative

relationship with God. We are called to live out and give expression in our lives to the words we say. 'We yield ourselves to God through prayer . . . we make ourselves available for God'⁴ and for God's purposes.

All this is followed by the words 'on earth as in heaven'.

These words sum up what will happen when God's name is hallowed, God's kingdom comes and God's will is done. Heaven will come to earth.

These words are what I am calling 'the hinge' between the first and second parts of the prayer.

Therefore, as we say this prayer, we express the earnest desire that the things we see in God may be established in the earth.

4.

HALLOWED BE YOUR NAME

No sooner have we uttered one word, saying one very beautiful thing about God, than we are uttering another which feels rather different.

Having established the absolute heart of things, that God is 'Our Father', and thus addressing God intimately and lovingly, the very next thing we say is a solemn acknowledgement of God's greatness and majesty.

Both are necessary. We address God with intimacy *and* adoration.

The one who is Father and Mother and very close to us is also the holy one, the creator and source of everything, the one whom it is impossible to imagine and who, by definition, must be beyond us, decked in inconceivable glory. 'If you can hold those two together,' says Tom Wright, 'you're already on the way to understanding what Christianity is all about.'[1]

We approach God as a child approaches its parents. At the same time, we say that God's name is holy. Which means we affirm the goodness, beauty and perfection of God, and we stand in continuity with the Jewish tradition that, as we have already discussed, knew God as the holy one, but did not and could not know the name of God.

Names are very important in the Bible.

Every name has a meaning, and a name can describe a person's identity.

Think of the new names that people are given as they discover a new identity and a new purpose through their relationship with God.

Jacob wrestles with God and is given a new name.

He longs to know God's name, and even though that name is not given, the very fact that he longs for it is the reason God blesses him.

Jesus gives Simon a new name. He is called Peter, 'the rock'.

As we discussed in Chapter 2, Moses also asks to know God's name, cunningly cosying up to God, and saying, 'If I come to the Israelites and say to them, "The God of your ancestors has sent me to you", and they ask me, "What is his name?" what shall I say to them?' (Exodus 3:13).

God replies with enigmatic beauty, 'I am who I am,' or, 'I will be what I will be.' Even the tense of these verbs is not clear.

In other words, God doesn't really answer the question at all, because as God is beyond us and unknowable by us, then also his name cannot be known. We *convert* it into a name, because it suits us, but the danger is that we end up domesticating God.

Hence, the Lord's Prayer sits in these two traditions, and all in a few words. It is why we need both intimacy and adoration.

God is Father, the Father of our Lord Jesus Christ who is teaching us this prayer, the one who makes access to God possible and available so that God is our Father too; but God is also the holy one who dwells outside us and beyond us, who is neither male nor female, who, as all the great mystics and the greatest theologians agree, can only really be described by what God isn't!

God *isn't* created.

God *isn't* human.

God *isn't* mortal.

God *isn't* limited by space and time.

God is what we are not, and yet at the same time we are made in God's image. Or to put it another way, as the great theologian Hans Urs von Balthasar said, 'God can't be captured by what we are, but somehow we can still reflect God.'[2] Or, Balthasar again, 'Things are both like God and unlike him, but God is not like things.'[3]

As Stephen Cherry puts it in his book on the Lord's Prayer, 'God is far too holy to have a name',[4] so we cannot turn 'hallowed' or 'holy' into God's name but receive this word to remind us of the inexpressible beauty, goodness and holiness of God – the beauty, goodness and holiness which becomes known and real in the person of Jesus.

It is almost as if language runs dry. Language, a *created* thing, the way we communicate and learn and understand, cannot describe the *uncreated* God. So, the uncreated God comes to us in Jesus Christ and speaks our language. All we can do in response is say how beautiful, holy and beyond us this is. Yet in Christ, God is with us. It is Christ who bridges the gap between unknowability and relatability. Both are in him. And in him, we meet with God.

The holiness that we see in Jesus is what we seek for ourselves. We seek to be holy as God is holy. We wish to live hallowed lives. ' . . . as he who called you is holy, be holy yourselves in all your conduct; for it is written, "You shall be holy, for I am holy"' says Peter (1 Peter 1:15–16, quoting Leviticus 11:44–45; 19:2).

Right relationship with God

Sometimes people who are new to the Christian faith, or experiencing Christian worship and prayer for the first time, are puzzled by how many of our hymns and prayers are filled with praise and admiration of God. Sometimes they are bemused by the titles we give to God. We call God 'holy'. We say that God is 'great' and 'strong'. We pray to 'Almighty God', 'Everlasting God', 'All-powerful Father' and so on.

'Your God must be very vain', they say. 'Why does God need to be praised all the time? Is God insecure?'

But the answer to this very reasonable question lies not with God, but with us – with our vanity and insecurities.

We don't call God 'holy', or address God as 'almighty' because God needs it.

It's because it helps us.

We put ourselves in perspective. We put ourselves in a right relationship with God. We hallow God.

God is not our equal.

God is not our possession.

God is the creator.

God is the one who is the source and origin of everything. Every breath we take, every word we utter, and absolutely everything we think and do, is contingent upon the ever-giving grace, goodness and ever-expending love of a good and holy God, the one whose constant goodness sustains the very universe itself.

We are, because God is.

And while we tend to put ourselves at the centre of the universe, it is to our own benefit to put God there instead: to allow God to take God's proper place at the heart of things – and in our hearts as well. This is why we praise God. This is why we say God's name is hallowed.

This is more than just putting a halo around God's name.[5] It is the acknowledgement of who God is and of who we are. It also changes us and expands our hearts. It puts us in right relationship with God – and with everything else that God has created.

Praise is good for us.

Learning to be thankful

In a recent book of mine, I used the example of clapping for the NHS during Covid as an example of this.[6] What started out as one thing – standing out on the streets with football rattles, saucepan lids and whistles, cheering for doctors and nurses – grew to become something larger and more beautiful: applauding and acknowledging all those whose sacrifice and labour supported us during those difficult days, including others who worked in emergency services, care home workers, delivery drivers and those who stocked the shelves in the supermarkets at night.

Suddenly, our understanding of whose work was essential and how we depended upon one another changed. And it was the praise that did it.

Once we started appreciating those whose work and sacrifice served us, even those we would never see or know, then we put ourselves into that new perspective of interdependence with one another, and with ourselves no longer at the centre.

This is holiness. It is the outward expression of an inward change in how we see ourselves and each other. It is an expression of our being the beloved children of a holy God.

And it is fuelled and shaped by praise. We live less for ourselves, and more for others.

The great spiritual writer Evelyn Underhill said that half the time we spend praying should be spent in adoration.[7] She believed this was hot-wired into us in the same way that St Augustine said that our hearts will always be restless until they find their rest in God. 'Our inheritance is God,' writes Robyn Wrigley Carr. 'God is our father and our home . . . we recognise God because we already carry in our hearts a rough sketch of his beloved countenance.' Alluding to one of the poems of John of the Cross, she continues, 'Looking into those deeps as into a quiet pool in a dark forest, we there find looking back at us the Face we implicitly long for and already know.'[8]

We are made in the image of this holy God. In Jesus, we have access to this holy God, and when we pray and praise, we enter into a new set of relationships, with God at the centre of our lives. This, as we are discovering, not only changes the way we understand God, but it changes the way we understand ourselves, and the way we see ourselves in relationship to others.

We begin the journey of living holy lives ourselves by living in relationship with God.

When Moses hears the name of God, even the enigmatic and unnameable name that he is given, Moses takes off his shoes.[9] God instructs him to do this because Moses is standing on holy ground. He is in the very presence of God.

We must do the same when we pray. And sometimes literally. Because when we pray, we are in communion with God. We are speaking with God. We are in relationship with God. The holy one has come to us in Jesus. The uncreated one who is the source of everything has entered into the creation and is now teaching us how to live, and even how to speak to God, so that the words we learn are the words that can shape our whole life. We grow into and become the very words we pray, what Tom Wright has described as a 'suit of clothes designed for us to wear in our full maturity', while recognising that at the moment, it is still a bit too big for us, that we still have some growing to do.[10]

5.

YOUR KINGDOM COME

The kingdom of God is not a place.

It has boundaries, but they run through human hearts.

It is under the rule of God, but it isn't a set of rules.

It is demonstrated in a certain way of living and a certain set of values.

It is, as Jesus himself put it, something so precious that you would sell everything to get it.

It is like a small measure of yeast, which is able to leaven all the dough.

It is like a tiny mustard seed, which grows to be the largest shrub of all.

It is a kingdom where the standards and protocols of the world are turned upside down. The poor, the disadvantaged and the lame are given the best seats in the house. Small children are considered to be the greatest of all.

Moreover, it is a kingdom without a king.

Although kingship is an important theme that runs through the whole biblical narrative and, indeed, can be helpful when we think of Jesus as the fulfilment of those Old Testament passages in Isaiah, where God's servant is called 'King of kings' and 'Lord of lords', actually, the rather stark revelation of God in Jesus Christ that we find in the

New Testament is that Jesus comes among us not as a king, but as a servant.[1]

Things just carry on being turned upside down. He is the one who washes people's feet, who waits on them, who tells his disciples that if they want to be great in the kingdom of heaven then they themselves must become the least of all, and a servant of all.

Therefore, when we pray 'your kingdom come', we are praying that we too might be part of this upside-down kingdom, live as servants to others after the example of Jesus, and demonstrate to the world a different set of attitudes and a different set of values to live by.

We believe that Jesus is a king. But he is a *servant* king, and his kingdom of justice, mercy and peace is to be established in human hearts, so that it overflows into the shaping and transforming of the kingdoms of the world.

Probably the best text for understanding this kingdom is the beatitudes.

Living as a child of God's kingdom

In Matthew's Gospel, right at the beginning of what we call the Sermon on the Mount, Jesus says this:

> 'Blessed are the poor in spirit, for theirs is the kingdom of heaven.
> Blessed are those who mourn, for they will be comforted.
> Blessed are the meek, for they will inherit the earth.
> Blessed are those who hunger and thirst for righteousness, for they will be filled.
> Blessed are the merciful, for they will receive mercy.

Blessed are the pure in heart, for they will see God.

Blessed are the peacemakers, for they will be called children of God.

Blessed are those who are persecuted for righteousness' sake, for theirs is the kingdom of heaven.

(MATTHEW 5:3–10)

A proper exploration of such an important text from the Bible deserves a book of its own, but for our purposes, let me suggest that one of the best ways of understanding the beatitudes is that they are a description of what it means to live as a child of the kingdom of God: what Robert Warren in his excellent book on the beatitudes calls 'characteristics of the children of the kingdom'.[2] That is, the attitudes, values and aspirations of those who want to live in God's kingdom, and *make* God's kingdom here on earth.

Straight away we can see that to live in the kingdom is about more than just following rules. The rules still exist: the moral code given to the people of Israel in the Ten Commandments still stands as the bedrock of the ethical life that we are meant to live by and serves as the code which marks and guides our behaviour, but the beatitudes say something more. They are not just about what we mustn't do, such as take God's name in vain, envy, slander, kill or steal. They are about how, in keeping these commandments, we are also called by Christ to go beyond them, and to live a different sort of life altogether – the life we see in Christ, who calls us to turn the other cheek, walk the extra mile, even to love our enemies.

If I keep the commandments, then I know I'm living a good life. If I follow the beatitudes, then I know I'm living a *Christ-like* life. Indeed, Jesus 'is the living embodiment of the beatitudes'. We can understand 'his whole life as a commentary on them'.[3]

So, let's look at them in just a little bit more detail.

Each beatitude has a threefold pattern. First there is the word 'blessed', which of course is a translation of a Greek word and could, in English, be equally well translated as 'happy'. Indeed, this is precisely what the New English Bible did in the 1960s.

It didn't go down well. But it revealed an important truth. This way of living is the way of happiness, fulfilment and joy.

Then, in each of the beatitudes there is a quality or an attitude, or what I'm going to call a *vocation,* something which we are called to adopt and inhabit: to be poor in spirit; to hunger and thirst for what is right; to be pure in heart. These are the things we have to take hold of and nurture in ourselves if we are to be like Christ, and even end up loving like Christ. Even, as I say, loving enemies as well.

Finally, there is a *promise*. Those who are merciful will receive mercy themselves. Those who are meek will inherit the earth.

However, we note that for both the opening beatitude – the vocation to be poor in spirit – and the final beatitude – the acknowledgement that living this way will mean not just misunderstanding, but persecution – the promise is the kingdom of heaven itself.

In fact, you could say that the middle six beatitudes promise an *aspect* of the kingdom that relates to the summons of the vocation itself, but the first and last beatitudes give you the *whole* kingdom now. Which means that although the beatitudes are meant to be read and received as one, the final promise is the inevitable outworking of what it means to live this way (as a child of the kingdom) and how it will lead to opposition with the powers and protocols of a world which still only looks to self, and is only too ready to build empires, protect them ruthlessly and advance them mercilessly. And the first beatitude may be a doorway into all the others.

So, what does it mean to be poor in spirit? And how does this relate to this important petition in the Lord's Prayer, 'your kingdom come'?

Blessed are the poor in spirit

To be poor in spirit must mean to be rich in the mercy and goodness of God, which only comes from knowing God and living in relationship with God, brooding upon God's word and being part of the worship of God's Church. And seeking, as we shall see in the next petition of the Lord's Prayer, to align our will with the will and purposes of God.

It therefore means not putting yourself at the centre of things. It means knowing you need resources outside of yourself. It means coming to God as a child. It means knowing your need of God and not taking yourself so seriously all the time.

Or to approach it another way, if you find it difficult to work out what some of the beatitudes mean – and several of them can be puzzling – then look to Jesus and see how he demonstrates the qualities and attitudes we find here.

Even Jesus, who is Son of God, is poor in spirit. Again and again in the Gospels we find occasions when Jesus slips away from the crowds (including his confused disciples) in order to enjoy intimacy with God and be renewed in his own understanding of his vocation. Here he receives the affirmation he needs. He rests in and is strengthened by the presence of God.

And so much of his teaching is about God's kingdom: what it looks like and how we will see it come among us. Moreover, he sends his disciples out to do the same. He tells them to heal and preach, to feed and bless (see Mark 6:7). And this is what he asks us to do today. It flows from a poverty of spirit, but it takes shape in lament for the injustices of the world – blessed are those who mourn; in seeking justice for the world – blessed are those who hunger and thirst for what is right; in a deep and gracious understanding of human failure – blessed are those who are merciful; in not just talking about peace, but being those who make it happen – blessed are the peacemakers.

If we say this prayer, and if we utter the astonishing three words 'your kingdom come', then we are committing ourselves to being part of this just and peaceful revolution.

We are no longer hungering and thirsting after what is best for us, but after what is best for the world, and especially for those who are most excluded.

We are crying out for a just distribution of the world's resources.

We are committing ourselves to inhabiting the world differently and taking seriously the existential challenge of climate crisis.

We are acknowledging that the poorest people in the world are paying the highest price.

We are saying that things could be different if we ourselves lived differently, established different priorities and acted less selfishly.

We are saying that war and violence, tyrants and dictators do not have the last word.

We are refusing to be cynical. We are invigorated by hope. Replenished by the purposes of God.

Although Jesus – and his disciples – were accused of turning the world upside down, they actually did no such thing. They turned it the right way up. It's just that we had got so used to it being the wrong way round that it looked strange when someone put it right.

But this is what we are praying for. A right-way-up world. And very specifically for those who suffer because of our wrong-way-round values. For the injustices, conflicts and pogroms of the world. For oppressed and oppressor. For abused and abuser. For the hateful and cynical as well as for the hopeful and the wise. For all who are in need. For refugees, asylum seekers, displaced people. For those who have been excluded from power, those who are without agency, those who are hungry, homeless, heartless, hopeless and poor. For all the left behind and forgotten people of the world. For those who have no one to pray for them.

In praying for all these situations and for all these people we look to what we recognise as the kingdom of God and our growing understanding of the will of God as a way of knowing what to pray for and what to hope for. We also recognise, as the beatitudes teach us, that even in those situations where we can do nothing more than cry out against what is wrong and hunger for what is right, it is still important to pray, because in praying we shape ourselves, our values and priorities, and learn to be part of the solution.

Our own lives can be an answer to the prayer we are uttering. Moreover, as with all prayer, as we align ourselves to the will of God, so God's energy and God's purposes, as we shall explore in the next section, are channelled through us. We become a source of God's blessing and comfort. We even learn how to love.

Tomorrow's life today

Finally, this might be the place to explore in a bit more detail something of the Jewish context in which Jesus lived and which shaped his praying. Jesus knew and practised the Jewish tradition of morning and evening prayers, which are, like our morning and evening prayers, rooted in the Psalms and in coming together as a community.

Jesus would have known the *Shema*, a Hebrew text consisting of three passages from the Pentateuch (Deuteronomy 6:4; 11:13–21; Numbers 15:37–41) and beginning 'Hear, O Israel, the Lord our God is one Lord'. It was an important part of Jewish morning and evening prayer and used as a confession of faith.

He would also have known the *Qaddish,* an old Jewish prayer in Aramaic, which is very similar to his own prayer, the one he taught his disciples. The *Qaddish* goes like this:

> Exalted and hallowed be his great name in the world,
> which he created according to his will.
> May he establish his kingdom in your lifetime and in your
>   days,
> and in the lifetime of the whole household of Israel,
> speedily and at a near time.[4]

But it is also significantly different from his own prayer.

When we compare the *Qaddish* with the Lord's Prayer, we see how Christ reinterprets and adds to it, even subverting its meaning.

First, Jesus introduces the intimate relational designation of 'Our Father'. God is still exalted and hallowed, but there is now a personal relationship. Jesus is the messianic shepherd gathering God's people together. Neither does Jesus speak about the whole household of Israel but makes this a prayer for the whole human race, all of whom can now be citizens of the kingdom he is proclaiming. The barriers between Jew and Gentile, which have mattered so much, are broken down. So are all other barriers as well.

Second, Jesus is showing us what an ideal community looks like. His inclusive and subversive table fellowship with, well, everyone is probably the greatest sign of this and the greatest irritation to his opponents. 'Why does he eat with tax-collectors and sinners?' was the complaint of the scribes (Mark 2:16). It was such shocking behaviour that it seems no further evidence of his delinquency was needed. Thus, we learn that the kingdom of God is for everyone.

Third, whereas the *Qaddish* asks that God may 'establish his kingdom in your lifetime and in your days', the Lord's Prayer is about that kingdom breaking in now; tomorrow's life today.

Just as prayer was so important for Jewish identity, so it was for Jesus and also for those who followed him. That is why Jesus gives us a prayer that forms us into a community that then lives out the prayer. We pray in great expectation of this coming kingdom, even when there is little we can actually do, or when it feels far off.

Finally, it is precisely because we don't have all the answers to our complex personal challenges or to the seemingly intractable challenges of the world that we continue to persevere in prayer. We continue to pray 'your kingdom come' and strive to be part of the answer ourselves by living differently and by standing up for those who are trodden down.

6.

YOUR WILL BE DONE

When I was ten years old my parents bought me a guitar for my birthday.

We were on holiday in Spain; the first time I had ever been abroad. We were with another family, and the dad in that family played the guitar. In fact, he bought himself a new guitar almost on day one of the holiday.

I was already taking piano lessons at the time so had a little bit of musical knowledge (though, sadly, no great aptitude for the piano and no great passion to practise). But the guitar enthralled me. I watched him play. He sat outside the tent strumming away. I sat outside the tent listening.

He taught me a few chords. Somewhere, I still have the bits of paper that he tore from his notebook to write out the shape of the chords.

Now, the guitar is probably the easiest instrument to play badly. Almost anyone with a reasonable sense of rhythm can soon learn how to play a few chords and start to make a half decent noise and even, if others are prepared to sing along, bang out what passes for a tune.

Like every instrument, skill, practice and commitment are required to play it well. But there also has to be desire. What made the guitar different from the piano for my ten-year-old self was that I *wanted* to play it. I wanted to play it all the time.

My birthday fell during the last few days of the holiday. I badgered my parents. Could I have a guitar for my birthday present? Fearful that it might be a fad, a sort of holiday romance that would wear off when I got home, they resisted. But I kept on at them. And with the helpful encouragement of their guitar-playing friend, they gave in. I got my first guitar.

Fifty-five years later, hardly a day goes by when I do not pick up my guitar and play. I never got to be much of a guitarist. But it's hard to think of any other thing that has given me such joy.

However, when I got home, armed with the few chords I'd already learned and eager to learn more, I quickly made an alarming and significant discovery. In order to play the guitar, you have first to know how to tune it! And in order to tune it, you need something else to tune it to.

The bass string of a guitar is tuned to E. Therefore, the standard way of tuning a guitar is to play E on a piano and then twist the knob at the end of the neck of the guitar where the E string is secured until the two notes, guitar and piano, are playing together. In tune with each other. If you have no piano (we did) then you need what's called a tuning fork which, when tapped, unfailingly produces its note in perfect pitch. These days you can buy electronic devices or download an app which does the same thing (and can even tell you when the string is in tune). But for the most part, all this is done by ear. You listen carefully to the note you need to reproduce and then adjust the string of the guitar accordingly. Once one string is in tune, all the others can be tuned from it.

The will of God, the good purposes of a good and loving

God, God's good purposes for the whole creation, for this earth and for everyone and everything in it, is like a single beautiful, clarifying note played and resonating throughout the universe. Everything else is tuned to it. Or at least it can be, and it should be. Making it so is the missionary challenge of the gospel and the invitation of God's kingdom.

Consequently, we observe and delight in the astonishing beauty and harmony of the created order, and find ourselves speaking about the 'music of the spheres'. We don't find it difficult to use a word like 'harmonious' to describe the universe.

If you have ever been to an orchestral concert, you will have noticed that as the orchestra comes on stage there is, at first, a cacophony of noise as each player tunes their instrument individually. Then the person playing the first violin ascends the stage. They play a single note. Everyone else in the orchestra tunes to it. From the unifying simplicity of this single note, the most amazingly beautiful and complex music is played.

The universe and all creation are held together in harmony by the single note of the will of God, played throughout the ages by the Holy Spirit and from which everything else is tuned. The music is indeed complex and beautiful. But it is held together; it is held in tune.

We are part of this. Our lives only find their full meaning and purpose, and we only find the fulfilment we long for, when we are in tune with God, playing our lives in tune and in time with God's life. This is what we mean by the will of God. God's good purposes for the world God has made, played out in our lives and participating joyfully in the great symphony of creation.

But unlike everything else in creation, we have a choice

about this. The trees, the rivers, the mountains and the stars are in tune with the God who made them because they just are. So too the simplest and most complex animals. An oyster or an octopus. Even animals that, like us, feel pain and even fear do not have the moral choices we have to choose to inflict pain for no reason, to create fear. We are different. We can hear the note of clarifying beauty and ignore it. Or stick our fingers in our ears. Or deny its existence. Or explain why it is just one of many notes and not to be taken so seriously. We can play our own music instead.

We will, in a later chapter, explore the consequences of what happens when we wilfully turn our back on the purposes of God, but for now let us focus on the beauty of God's will and how tuning our lives to the life of God as we see lived out so perfectly in Jesus is not only the best way for the world itself to know peace and joy, it's what's best for us as well. As St Augustine said, our hearts are restless till they find their rest in God.

God's will gives us the yardstick, the plumb-line (and the tuning fork) whereby we can measure life.

It is liberating. We can be set free from thinking that our own will and our own stubborn and selfish desires are the be all and end all of life.

We again take hold of that fundamental Christian lesson that life is supposed to be lived in harmony with others. Primarily with God but also with each other.

Tuning our hearts to the heart of God

When we say 'your kingdom come, your will be done', we are committing ourselves to listening out and learning from the will of God: the heart of God speaks to our heart and shapes our will. We test our lives, not against our own will and the things we think we want for ourselves, but against what God teaches us, particularly in Scripture and through the life of Jesus, about how life should be lived. About what is right and what is wrong. And about the higher calling to live unselfishly and sacrificially for the good of everyone. We get in tune.

But we can't pretend this is easy. The beginning of all sinfulness is the insistence on our own will. Even Jesus struggled with this. In Gethsemane, knowing that Judas had betrayed him, that the powers who were set against him were encircling him, and that death was very near, Jesus prayed in agony and desperation, so much so that Luke's Gospel tells us that 'his sweat became like great drops of blood falling down on the ground' (Luke 22:44). 'Abba, Father,' he prays, 'for you all things are possible; remove this cup from me.' Out of this all-too-human struggle Jesus' prayer ends with a profound and moving echo of the Lord's Prayer: 'My Father, if it is possible, let this cup pass from me . . . if this cannot pass unless I drink it, *your will be done*' (Matthew 26:39, 42, my italics).

This is why we persist with the Lord's Prayer. We learn the centrality and importance of these words. We long for God's kingdom to come; but we discover, and often through suffering, that God's kingdom can only come if God's will is done.

This tells us something vitally important for *all* prayer. Something about which we often get muddled. Prayer is not an attempt to change God's mind. Listening in to some people's prayers, you could be forgiven for thinking this is what we are doing – trying to persuade God about something – because so much of our prayer is asking for stuff. In fact, for many, many Christians, their prayer never gets much beyond this.

It's not that it's wrong to ask things of God. Jesus himself says, 'Ask, and it will be given to you . . . knock, and the door will be opened' (Matthew 7:7). But we can't bargain with God. Prayer is not a transaction. When we ask for things, we do it knowing that at the heart of the prayer Jesus himself said and taught us are these words: 'Your will be done'. So, when we pray for those we know who are ill, or those we love who are dying, or for those who are hungry or homeless, or for any of the great challenges facing the world, we are bringing these people and these things into the presence of God, asking that God will do what is right and best for them. That God's will may be done, not ours.

This is enormously hard. Of course we want what we think is best. If someone we know is ill, we want them to get better. If someone we love is dying, we want them to live. But prayer can never be this straightforward. As we have already noted, we live in a world where we are made with freedom and choice. This is also a world where we know that there is illness and death. Even though Jesus healed many people, and asks us to do the same, this does not mean that in this life we won't be ill again and that we won't one day die. Even Lazarus, whom Jesus famously raised from the dead, resumed his life on earth in the knowledge that he would have to die all over again.

So of course we bring these things to God. Of course we cry out to God. Of course we long for God to act in our lives and in the lives of those we love, and to bring peace on earth. But we also know that in so many of these situations God will answer our prayers by making us the people who live differently and become peacemakers and sources of blessing. We will, as I said in the last chapter, become the answer to our own prayers.

Therefore, like the words that run through a stick of rock so that wherever you break it open it says the same thing, the words 'your will be done' run through the heart of all Christian prayer, as they did for Jesus' own praying.

Sometimes amazing and inexplicable things happen which are beyond our understanding, and we experience what we can only describe as miraculous intervention. In these situations, we are filled with glorious and stupefied thanksgiving.

But often they don't happen. And one day each of us will die.

The truth is we do not know how God will answer our prayer. In fact, even the word 'answer' might be a symptom of approaching prayer in the wrong way. As if it were a question to God, rather than God's question to us. But we do know, because we see it in Jesus, that God is not indifferent or uninterested in our suffering and in the heartbreaking travails of the world. Far from it. God is deeply committed. Passionately involved. Painfully extended.

But this is the world we have. Perhaps the only world where creatures like us could emerge who, because we are able to choose and because we are neither prevented from doing what is wrong nor programmed to do what is right, are also able to love. Because love can only be love if it is free.

In this world of freedom, beauty, moral choice and love there are also startling and terrible things, such as the consequences of our failing to love and our failing to follow the will of God: the things we do to each other and the world which erupt into the horrors of warfare, which create climate crisis, which accept the unacceptable sufferings of children born into poverty, which acquiesce with inequality. Then there are the so-called 'natural disasters' of earthquake and flood, of cancer and dementia and death itself.

This is the world we have, and without Jesus it really would make no sense at all, and we could hardly be blamed for pulling up the drawbridge, doing the best to preserve what we have and postponing the inevitabilities of diminishment and death for as long as possible.

But Jesus *has* come into the world. He has come to show the world that God loves us, and that God cares for the creation God made. And in Jesus, God becomes human, and experiences the suffering and death that we experience.

He teaches us to pray. He says that when we pray, we use these words. Therefore, the words 'your will be done' are perhaps the most important ones of all. They come from the broken heart of Jesus, who wept at the tomb of his friend Lazarus, because he too did not want it to be this way. But he is saying to us that in the midst of the brokenness and fallenness of the world, and with all the misery that is caused by human failing (but also because this is just the way the world is), then when we pray, we of course bring everything to God but at the same time say, 'God's will be done.'

Opening our hearts to the presence and the purposes of God

Jesus did not come into the world only to experience what the world is like, but to redeem the world.

He has become what we are, so that we can become what he is. By his death and resurrection, he shows us that death and evil do not have the last word.

We pray 'your will be done' in the sure and certain hope

of the resurrection to eternal life, knowing that despite the travails and sufferings of this life, ultimately God's will is that we should all be raised to life in Christ. We always pray in this great hope. Which also means that for each of us as individuals, and for those we love, when we do come to the end of our lives on earth, the greatest prayer and the greatest hope is that God's will may be done *through our dying*, as we go to that place Jesus has prepared for those who love him.[1]

Therefore, when we pray, we are not trying to change God's mind. We are not trying to persuade God to do things God might not want to do. We are not trying to impose our will upon the will of God. Rather, we are placing ourselves in right relationship with God as those who are children of God, and as those who would have nothing without God – and we let God change our mind.

Prayer, we might even say, is not what we say to God, but what God says to us. We are open to the presence of God. We listen out for the hopeful note and steadfast certainty of God's will. And knowing that this life is brief and full of sadness, we tune ourselves to God. We commit ourselves to participating with God in God's purposes for the world.

What we tend to *call* prayer, the stuff we quite naturally bring to God and all the things we ask of God, is simply our response to all that God gives us in Jesus and by the Spirit, and what he teaches us about how we should live our lives. Prayer is what God does in us by the Spirit, singing the love song that he has made known to Jesus deep in the heart of our being. In this way the words of prayer Jesus taught his friends become our words; they are spoken with our lips and they rest in our hearts, so that whatever happens in life, and even at the hour of our death, we know we are held and loved by God, and in tune with God, and being made ready for the music of heaven.

As Stephen Cherry puts it, we should not be 'neutral about God's will . . . we should make it our own'.[2]

7.

ON EARTH AS IN HEAVEN

For about forty years, my mother sang each year in the 'scratch' performance of Handel's *Messiah* at the Royal Albert Hall. It is a great pre-Christmas annual event and about three quarters of the Albert Hall is taken up by this huge put-together-on-the-day choir made up of singers from amateur choirs up and down the country and from all over the world. One small wedge of seating is left for a much smaller than usual audience. For many of those forty years I sat in the audience.

The orchestra and the soloists are of the highest standard. The choir is magnificent and enthusiastic. What it lacks in polish is more than made up for in zest, gusto and volume. When the choir rise to sing the first chorus – hundreds and hundreds of them – it is thrilling and inspiring.

And what a piece of music. The libretto for the oratorio is a tapestry of Scripture. Taken from the prophet Isaiah, the opening word is 'Comfort'. 'Comfort ye, comfort ye my people, saith your God' (Isaiah 40:1, KJV).

This is interesting and instructive. The story of the Messiah and the story of the Christian faith is of God's comforting in Jesus Christ. And to comfort means to strengthen.

A high point of *Messiah* is one of the few pieces of

classical music just about everybody knows: the very famous Hallelujah chorus. It is a great, climactic shout of joyful and victorious praise.

However, about two thirds of the way through, there is a shift in the music. For a moment its note of triumph is offset by a moment of profound solemnity as the chorus sings these words from the book of Revelation: 'The kingdom of this world is become the kingdom of our God and of his Christ' (Revelation 11:15).

This one verse from Scripture sums up much of what we have been talking about in this part of the book. And I like the fact that it is something to be sung about. This itself echoes the music of the heavens, the song of the angels, and that single note from God to which the whole universe is tuned. All God's purposes, the whole biblical narrative and the whole Christian faith are about the work of God, which is to restore all things in Christ so that the kingdoms of this world become the kingdoms of God. These same ideas are summed up even more succinctly in the Lord's Prayer itself: 'Your kingdom come on earth as in heaven.'

To which I think we can naturally deduce: your will be done *on earth as in heaven*; your name be hallowed *on earth as in heaven*.

In Christ, God is gathering everything together into a new creation.

In Christ, everything about heaven comes to fill the earth, like light flooding a darkened room. This light reveals and illuminates everything. Thus, everything earthly is transformed so as to be heavenly, so as to bear the currency of the kingdom of God.

For Christians, heaven can never simply be somewhere else. Earth is not invaded or replaced by heaven. We pray for 'God's name, kingdom and will to come on earth *like* it is in heaven, not for heaven to come to earth as such. Earth as a realm or sphere of activity has its own creaturely integrity. The kingdom of Christ comes to fill it (like light fills a room) so that it retains the dignity of its character while also being transformed and suffused by the indwelling presence of God – much as the humanity of Jesus was fully retained but also fully in union with the divinity of the Son.'[1] These words, cried out in the middle of the Hallelujah chorus, are part of this much larger narrative in the book of Revelation, which is speaking of a new creation, a new heaven and a new earth.

This is what Jesus believed. This is what he taught. This is what we affirm when we say the Lord's Prayer. It is, therefore, this that shapes our praying and our living. 'God's kingdom has been launched on earth as in heaven, and the way it will happen is by God working through people like us,' says Tom Wright.[2]

Joining in with the mission of God

A few years ago, a piece of footage of people singing the Hallelujah chorus became something of an internet sensation. It was one of those flash mob, pop-up events. It got millions of views.

If I remember correctly, it begins in a crowded shopping centre. People are milling around. There are cafés and restaurants. People are sitting at tables, eating and chatting. Others are shopping, looking in windows, going about their business.

Then someone stands up.

From somewhere – a recording? – we hear an organ play.

The person starts to sing. The opening line of the Hallelujah chorus. Just that repeated word: 'Hallelujah'.

Then someone else from across the shopping mall stands and echoes back that single word. 'Hallelujah.'

At an adjacent table, others stand and join in.

Then more and more.

People who are passing by stop to enjoy the music.

A parent reaches out for their child's hand.

An elderly woman wipes a tear from her eye.

I myself remember watching it for the first time and weeping.

Others rise up.

The music builds and builds.

Soon, amid the ordinariness of everyday life, and arising from it seemingly without any prearrangement or rehearsal, as if it's just happening as naturally as the rays of the sun and the movement of the breeze, a whole choir has emerged, has risen out of the crowd, and has, at the same time, made the crowd into something else, and is singing this great chorus of praise.

In this beautiful bit of impromptu, but of course actually very carefully prepared, musical theatre we see a lived-out demonstration of what it means for the kingdom of this world to become the kingdom of our God and of his Christ, and of the world hearing, as if for the first time, the music of God: joining in and being deeply moved by it. Moved to tears, and so moved that we long to hold the hands of those we love, because we see, in the ordinariness of everyday life, something bigger and more beautiful and more meaningful breaking in and breaking out. The world as it is is transformed into the world as it could be.

Every time we say the Lord's Prayer, we are pledging

ourselves to this kind of future; that God's kingdom may break through and break out, on earth as it is in heaven.

These three great praises to the God who is 'Our Father' – your name be hallowed, your kingdom come, your will be done – are the song and the pledges of those of us who want to live the life of heaven now and build the life of heaven in the kingdoms of the world. And with this beautiful music and its enormous challenge ringing in our ears the prayer turns from heaven to earth, from consideration of God and the purposes of God, to how we live our lives on earth.

As I said earlier, as Jesus introduces the Lord's Prayer in Matthew's Gospel, he says clearly that 'your Father knows what you need before you ask him' (Matthew 6:8). To which we retort, 'So why are we bothering to ask him?' Well, the answer is because we don't know what we need. Or we only *think* we know what we need. But now we will learn that in the life of heaven on earth there are three humble petitions that we need to make, and these three things will shape a Christian life, on earth as it is in heaven. The Lord's Prayer is 'an education in desire'.[3]

Part Three

THREE HUMBLE REQUESTS

It is right that we start with God before thinking of ourselves. But we then inevitably move into the focus of God's purposes for us . . .

KENNETH STEVENSON[1]

The three declarations that form the first part of the Lord's Prayer are followed by three humble requests, and only three. This alone demonstrates how the Lord's Prayer teaches us what we should be asking from God. As Pope Francis has put it, the three requests that complete the prayer 'express our fundamental needs: bread, forgiveness, and help in temptation'.[2]

Writing in 1649, Jeremy Taylor, one of the greatest Anglican spiritual writers, observed that the petitions of the Lord's Prayer suggest the different relationships we have with God. In these three, we come as a 'necessitous beggar' asking for bread; as a sinner, 'a penitent servant' asking forgiveness; as a person 'in affliction and danger' longing for safety.[3]

Observing the symmetry and structure of the prayer in Matthew's version, John Dominic Crossan notes how the first three petitions centre around the word 'your', referring directly to God, while the second three petitions centre around the word 'our', referring directly to 'us' and what we need from God and how the world may be ordered as God intends.

Here is another one of his more literal translations which helpfully makes the point.

The first half of the prayer is about God's *divinity* and God's life, as it were, *in heaven*.

The second half is about our *humanity*, and therefore is concerned with what happens *on earth*.

Be hallowed	YOUR name	Give US this day OUR daily bread.
Be come	YOUR kingdom	Forgive us OUR debts as we have forgiven etc.
Be done	YOUR will	Do not lead US into temptation . . . deliver US from evil[4]

As we move into this part of the prayer, we will find ourselves deeply challenged. We are now very definitely praying that God's will be done in very real bits of our life. We are considering what we actually need, how we actually deal with others and whether we may end up revelling in the temptations this life has to offer and turning our back on God. As is always the case, things get more difficult when we turn from the general to the very particular.

This is how Jesus teaches us. Our faith is worked out in the very specific ways we live our lives each day. Let me offer a very big 'for instance'. Jesus doesn't just tell us to love everyone. Such a generalised, abstract and non-specific love may seem relatively easy. No, he asks us to love our neighbour. He asks us to love the very particular people we live with and mix with each day. And because we go on saying 'us' and 'our', this includes all the particular, beloved people of the world who are our sisters and brothers.

'Your kingdom come, your will be done on earth as in heaven' is now going to be worked out in some very practical ways.

8.

GIVE US TODAY OUR DAILY BREAD

A few years ago, enjoying the precious gift of a sabbatical that all stipendiary clergy in the Church of England are offered every ten years, I walked a large section of the *Camino del Norte* in northern Spain from Santander to Santiago. It took about a month.

The guidebooks and websites that I consulted before setting off advised me to keep my rucksack down to 9 kg if at all possible, implying that I probably wouldn't be able to manage this, but it was something to aim for.

As I set off, I weighed my rucksack. It was just over 9 kg. I was pleased with myself. I was travelling light.

However, after a few days on the road, not only was that 9 kg feeling heavier and heavier, but I also realised I had too much stuff with me. For instance, I had packed three pairs of socks, three pairs of knickers and three shirts. But I only needed two. Wash one, wear one. Wash one, wear one.

This was an astonishing revelation. What I actually needed was so little; and to spend a month with everything I needed carried on my back, plus the sobering discovery that even though my possessions were now so few, I still carried things

I didn't need, was an education in need and a further education in desire.

This is what the Lord's Prayer teaches us. And it was on that very long walk across northern Spain that I properly learned this lesson. Though, inevitably, I am still not good at putting it into practice in most areas of my life.

To pray 'Give us today our daily bread' invites us to reflect upon the relationship between *need* and *desire*, about how we might find a way of being satisfied with what we need, not wanting more all the time; and at the same time *educate* our desires and motivations so that it is not only by acquiring more that they find satisfaction. Especially at the expense of others, or at an unacceptable cost to the planet itself.

It also invites us to reflect on what our world might look like if it were ordered around the provision of daily bread for everyone, and how I might learn to stop expecting more than my share. Because the Lord's Prayer is about *God's* will and *God's* kingdom, and the things of heaven being manifest in the earth.

Or, to put it another way: what does 'enough' look like?

I am painfully aware that I have too much. I am painfully aware that there are so many people in the world – the vast majority! – who have so little.

We live in a world of deepening poverty, and we can see that poverty on our own streets, those living without a home being just the visible tip of a chilling iceberg of need, inequality, disappointment and despair.

For the first time in ages, we have seen the gap between rich and poor increasing in the UK. Even before the Covid pandemic, the wealth of the top 10 per cent of the population had increased by 11 per cent, whereas that of the bottom 10 per cent increased by just 3 per cent.[1] Regional variations are even more stark. Household wealth in the south-east is more than twice as high as the north-east.

The Children's Society reckons that four million children live in poverty. That's a third of all children living in the UK, the equivalent of nine children in an average classroom.[2] No wonder food banks have become such a feature of contemporary Britain.

Sometimes the Church has spoken about having a bias to the poor, making sure that every decision we make is judged by its impact on those who are most deprived and most underprivileged. It requires us to speak of the common good, which, as Pope Francis describes, 'is the good we all share in, the good of the people as a whole, as well as the good we hold in common that should be for all'.[3]

The worldwide Covid pandemic has made things worse. Poorer communities suffered disproportionately.

However, it has also revealed an interconnectedness. It may have been easier for wealthier people and richer nations to shield themselves from Covid, but we also found out that the pandemic could only be dealt with *anywhere* by being dealt with *everywhere*. When we failed to share the vaccine, new strains of the virus mutated in poorer parts of the world and then returned to afflict us, defying the very vaccines we had kept for ourselves.

Christians should not be surprised by this. Nor anyone who says a prayer beginning 'Our Father'. Walls and barriers do not create the security they promise, only isolation and fear. Paradoxically, as Jesus shows us, knocking them down is usually the answer.

We therefore need economic systems and ethical frameworks that demonstrate solidarity with each other as one humanity inhabiting one world and therefore bound together by bonds of mutual love; everything that is expressed by simply saying, 'Our Father . . . your kingdom come.'

However, political and economic thinking rarely includes discussion of the common good. People themselves are usually spoken about as either employees or consumers. The market decides. There is only one incentive in society: financial growth and accumulation of financial wealth.

Many are left behind, especially in the developing world, but even in our own inner cities and outer estates. This approach narrows the moral perspective which the Lord's Prayer so gloriously opens up. We end up in a world where, as someone has put it, we know the price of everything, but the value of nothing. As Pope Francis says: 'The free market is anything but free for huge numbers of people, above all for the poor, who end up with little or no choice in practice . . . solidarity (with the poor) is not sharing the crumbs from the table, but to make space at the table for everyone.'[4]

Which brings us back to bread. And to the uncomfortable and unfashionable concept of 'enough'. What we have is *more* than enough and an economic system built upon maintaining our market-driven need to *want* more than enough.

Advertising endlessly massages our desires. Sophisticated algorithms mine our data, and Amazon, Google and Facebook tell us what we need and how to buy it cheaply. So we say that we *need* this holiday. Or we *need* a new pair of jeans, or a third, fourth or fifth outfit; or we *need* a new car. What we mean is that we *want* those things, but we have so blurred the lines between need and desire that we no longer even notice it exists. Meanwhile, because our whole system depends on it, any drop in spending is reported as tragedy.

The real tragedy is the very heavy price that is being paid by the poorest people of the world, and also, of course, by the planet itself. The escalating climate crisis which threatens to engulf the world is a direct consequence of our failure to say this bit of the Lord's Prayer and mean it. We want to make ourselves an exception. We want more than enough.

Learning what enough looks like

In his book *What Money Can't Buy: The Moral Limits of Markets*, Michael J. Sandal charts the expansion of markets and of market values into spheres of life where they don't really belong. 'We have drifted from *having* a market economy to *being* a market society,' he says.[5] Whereas a market economy is a valuable and effective tool for organising productive activity, a market society is a way of life where market values – the idea that everything can be bought or sold and with it the commodification of everything – seep into every aspect of life.

He cites an alarming number of examples, from the proliferation of 'for-profit' schools, hospitals and even prisons to the outsourcing of war to private military contractors and public police forces being replaced by private security firms, the outsourcing of pregnancy to surrogate mothers in the developing world and the buying and selling of the right to pollute.

Citizens become consumers. Everything has a price. Even things like blood and friendship, which should be priceless, are bought and sold.

To say that we need to discover what 'enough' looks like is, therefore, also to say we have *had enough* of this commodification of life and the ethical damage it has done. We want to reset the compass.

Looking at the very word 'economy' may be a good place to begin.

In my recent book *Dear England* I explored the meaning of the word 'economy'. It comes from two Greek words: *oikos*, meaning 'household', and *nomos*, meaning 'law'. So, the literal meaning is 'the law of the household'. Furthermore, *nomos* is from another Greek word, *nemein*, meaning 'to distribute', indicating that law and justice have something to do with fair distribution.

A good economy is meant to be like a well-run household.[6] And though most of us do not claim a great understanding of economics (and I sometimes think that economists and the politicians they advise would prefer to keep it that way) we do know what a well-run household should be like. Everyone is treated equally and fairly. In a family – a household – it would be unthinkable that at the dinner table some were fed while others went hungry.

This approach to life – and economics – is sometimes called distributive justice. It is a theme that runs through the Bible, especially in the books of the Old Testament prophets, who rage against the people of Israel, saying that what God wants is not their worship and their festivals, but justice – a justice that can only come when we recognise that we inhabit this planet together with mutual responsibility to one another and to the land itself.

But we don't tend to think about justice in this distributive way. Often, we just think of it as retribution; as settling a score, not building a different future; still less, cancelling a debt.

God's vision is bigger and more positive. Arising from its Jewish roots, the Christian tradition has always believed that to be just, as God is just, means to distribute things fairly.

When the people of Israel were liberated from slavery in Egypt, God fed them with manna from heaven. Everyone had enough. But no one had more than enough. And, because they had been slaves themselves, the good stewardship of the household of God's earth extended to others, especially those who were strangers and outcasts. Through a beautiful and complex system of Sabbath rest and jubilee this extended to the land itself. Every year a portion of the harvest was left for the poor and the stranger. Every seventh year the land itself rested. Every fiftieth year, that is after 'seven times seven' years, there was a kind of super-Sabbath for the land where not only did the land rest, but debts were cancelled. The reason? 'The land is mine,' says God.

This suggests a model of stewardship, not ownership, for our ordering of the world. God requires us to share what we have with those who are in need.

We do not own the land. We must treat it fairly, preserve its fertility, and share its goodness. Sabbath rest, it turns out, is not just a useful reminder that mindfulness is good for us (and has been around for quite a while!) but a political act: an injunction to good and just stewardship of the world, where we strive for the common good, not just individual gain. Therefore, the measure for enough is the measure of the needs of the poor and the needs of the planet, not just the imagined or manufactured needs of a market economy.

From the perspective of the Lord's Prayer, fair distribution and the good stewardship that allows the earth itself to breathe and rest and maintain its fertile goodness, should be the yardstick. 'Give us our daily bread' means a fair distribution of food, but also a fair distribution of security; a fair distribution of land, of education, of access to health, of opportunity, and even access to justice itself. These things no longer just go to those who can pay for them.

Just as a good household looks after and works for the benefit of all its members, would not consider doing otherwise and would happily make the sacrifices that are necessary to ensure that the weakest and most vulnerable are not left out, so should a good society. Our first responsibility is that everyone has their daily bread. This will necessarily mean some of us having less. But it won't mean creating less wealth. On the contrary we need more and more people invested in just and sustainable development.

Paradoxically, this is also an area where the poor themselves may show leadership. Both in the UK and around the world, I have always been humbled and amazed by the sacrifices I see some of the poorest people make on behalf of one another and in the service of a greater good. Often the wealthier you are, the more insulated your life becomes, leaving you less able to see a different way of living, or even notice the harm your isolation is doing, not least to yourself.

I have had the enormous and life-changing privilege of receiving hospitality from unimaginably poor, nomadic people in northern Kenya living through a second year of drought. I have seen shanty town congregations giving generously to charity in ways that would deeply shame our own priorities. I have known outer estate parishes in this country giving more generously than leafy suburbs.

In sub-Saharan Africa and in Pacific island communities, whose bishops and people I have met, their more interdependent ways of living with each other and with the land are threatened by a climate crisis that they have had little part in creating. And it might be this climate crisis, even more than

Covid, that will force us to rethink and to imagine a different kind of economic life where we say, 'Enough!' to some of our current models and begin to work out what living *with enough* looks like and what its implications will be.

We have known for many years that we must find a carbon neutral way of inhabiting this planet. Progress towards this vital and elementary goal is shockingly slow. We continue to do the things we know are causing the problem, hoping that new technology will advance quickly enough to offset our moral, political and economic shortcomings.

Technology may save us. But it may not. In the meantime, we must take other measures.

Introducing the concept of 'enough' – both that we've *had* enough of a certain way of doing things and that we must learn to *live with* enough now – may be our best way forward, changing our behaviour, curbing our carbon-guzzling habits and cultivating restraint and a culture of shared sacrifice.

A global market with the right to pollute undermines this at every turn. It is the modern-day equivalent of indulgences, the payments sinners paid in the medieval church to offset their sinfulness. They didn't work then, and right now they only obscure the challenge facing us and let us off the hook of our moral responsibilities to each other and to the planet.

The new ethic that we need is described by Jonathan Porritt as 'an evolved, intelligent and elegant form of capitalism that puts the Earth at its very centre (as our one and only world) and ensures that all people are its beneficiaries'.[7] He defines sustainable development as 'a dynamic process which enables all people to realize their potential and to improve their quality of life in ways which simultaneously protect and enhance the Earth's life-support systems'.

Or we might say, 'Your kingdom come on earth as in

heaven. Give us today our daily bread, and stop us, prevent us, from wanting more than our share.'

Sustaining the life of the earth

The Christian tradition helps us to speak naturally of the whole cosmos as a character in the story of creation and redemption, not a backdrop or a stage set. We don't live *on* the world, but *in* the world. We are part of the creation. We are also its stewards. We are children of God and charged by God to work for – another petition in the Lord's Prayer – God's rule *in* earth as *in* heaven. We can, therefore, never use the world as if it were our possession. Or ignore it, as if it didn't matter. The world, which is God's creation and of which we are part, is to be cherished, responded to, cared for and loved. It belongs to all of us. Its good ordering and well-being are tied up with our own.

Interestingly, if you look at the English version of the Lord's Prayer that has been used more than any other down the centuries, which is the one you will find in the 1662 Book of Common Prayer, it does say '*in* earth as in heaven'. Neither, I think, was there ever any conscious decision to change this. Even before the liturgical revisions of the twentieth century cast the prayer in contemporary English, we had started to say '*on* earth' instead. Perhaps it unconsciously echoes the deep malaise of the climate emergency that we have created, because at some point in the last two hundred years we did stop believing we lived in the earth, and thought we lived on it instead. We stopped thinking of ourselves as being part of the creation, and interdependent with all the other forms of life which make up the abundant and beautiful complexity of life on earth. We began to treat it as a possession we could plunder and use as we like.

This has to change. Praying earnestly each day, 'Give us our daily bread,' will help.

Daily bread should be a human right. 'Market choices are not free choices if some people are desperately poor or lack the ability to bargain on free terms.'⁸ Why else would some people sell their kidneys? Or even their children?

Thinking about 'enough' helps us to begin to reimagine what our world could be.

Returning to the two biblical texts of the prayer, both Matthew and Luke's versions make this point in different ways.

In Matthew's version Jesus speaks about daily bread for today (Matthew 6:11). In Luke's version Jesus says, 'Give us *each day* our daily bread' (Luke 11:3, my italics).

These small differences become more interesting when we consider the word 'daily'. The Greek word is *epiousios*. It doesn't appear anywhere else in the New Testament. It is usually translated as 'daily' but probably means more than this. Some ancient commentators translated it as 'bread of essential being' or 'bread for the coming day', a kind of 'anticipation of the banquet of heaven bread', much more like the bread we receive in Holy Communion.⁹ So a richer translation might be, 'Give us today our bread for tomorrow.'

'The bread we pray for,' writes Kenneth Stevenson, 'is the bread of the kingdom in all its totality, physical, spiritual, unconventional and therefore eucharistic in every possible sense.'¹⁰ It is about actual bread, but also the bread of heaven.

In Matthew the emphasis is on the life of tomorrow breaking into today. In Luke it is the sustenance we need and ask for each day.

Both meanings are important. Crossan explains it this way: 'Enough for today, but also with assurance of the same tomorrow. It is a request that "our daily bread" be never again exceptional, or conditional, as in the past, but always normal and unconditional in the present and the future.'[11]

Moreover, it is in the Eucharist, where we say the Lord's Prayer as almost our last words before receiving Communion, that these truths come together, so that the Eucharist itself becomes an acted parable of the coming kingdom. All have an equal place around the Lord's table. All are fed.

With his usual profound simplicity, Pope Francis helps us remember that this is practical and everyday. It is and should be available to everyone, the daily bread of daily life *and* the bread of heaven. If someone is hungry and thirsty for these things, then *I am responsible.* 'I cannot delegate this,' he says. 'This person needs me: my help, my words, my efforts. We are in this together.'[12]

He goes on: 'Would it be good for us to linger a bit over this petition and to think about how many people do not have bread?'[13]

The feast as well as the fast

There is another side to the coin. For another major theme in Christianity is abundance.

Five thousand people are fed, and the disciples gather up twelve baskets of leftovers.

The fishermen haul in a catch that is so astonishingly large their nets start breaking.

An already inebriated assembly of wedding guests are given the very last thing they actually need, a ridiculously large supply of additional alcohol – and not just any old plonk, but 180 gallons of the very finest vintage!

How do we fit such abundance into a concept of living with enough? And even though I didn't need that third pair of socks and third shirt, there were other things I carried in my rucksack that were hugely precious and added to the weight, but I would have clung on to even if my last pair of socks proved too much to carry. These included the photograph of those I love; the holding cross that I gripped tightly through the darker and more difficult parts of the journey; the bar of chocolate that I didn't really need, though could justify as a good source for the necessary replenishing of energy, but which felt like a little luxury, and therefore kept me going in ways which were not just about the efficient delivery of calories. And that's before I get on to all the very lovely, but unnecessary, beer I drank each evening.

Perhaps we need another concept from the Christian tradition to place alongside the concept of enough: the interrelationship between feasting and fasting.

Not only does our society fail to acknowledge the common good and distribute things fairly as in a well-run household, we tolerate and knowingly enable certain parts of society to live with huge excess while others don't have enough. The wealth does not trickle down. Well, not much. This is where walls do work. They create a dam that keeps wealth in.

For some parts of the world and for some people in it, it is always feast.

For others, it is always fast.

It is in the rebalancing of this that we will discover not only a fair and equitable way of inhabiting the world, but also a joyful one. In fact, can one really enjoy the feast if there is no fast to precede it? And if others have nothing, how good does my plenty actually taste?

We need to learn how to do both, and build a world where both are available for everyone: to feast and to fast; to learn what enough looks like; and also, to celebrate.

With this we will recover and enjoy other disciplines that we have lost: things like saving, mending, making and recycling.

Second-hand really is pre-loved.

'Enough' is not miserable. I will have my share. But it will be more lovely because what I used to have just for myself is now shared with others. Moreover, finding contentment in enough, and making the changes to our lifestyles that living with enough demands, come from a deep awareness that God will provide for us, that God's love is sufficient for us, and that God will give us our basic needs and be with us in times of difficulty and need.

Mark Powley argues that Christianity outlasted and outshone the Roman Empire partly because of its resistance of the dominant system. This was embodied by an image of 'a shepherd carrying the weak rather than a soldier crushing them'.[14] We need a similar resistance movement against unchecked consumerism today and the monopolies that drive it.

We might also discover that the disciplines of the fast, whereby the planet itself is given a breather, and those excesses that we no longer permit ourselves to have each day, enable a more equitable sharing of resources across the world and make the feast even more enjoyable.

Finally, another thing I learned on the *Camino* was to do with receiving. There were days when I didn't have enough myself. On the first three days of my pilgrimage, I landed up in small villages where the shops were closed and there was no restaurant. All I had to eat in the evenings was bar snacks. This was enforced fasting. On the third evening I was getting quite depressed about this, concluding that I just had to carry a lot more food with me than the bar of chocolate, bag of peanuts and banana that were my emergency rations. The village I was staying in did have quite a large bar, but there didn't seem to be a restaurant. Fearing another day without a proper meal and reflecting on the irony that although I was expending more calories each day than had probably been the case since I was a teenager, I wasn't taking enough on and that usually, and for most of my adult life, it had been the other way round, I sat and nursed my beer. I munched on a bag of nuts. Then, at the table next to me where two other pilgrims were sitting, great plates of paella were set down. I asked them how they had managed to order the food, since there was no one else eating, no sign of a menu and no indication that meals were available. 'You just ask,' they told me. 'Tell them you are a pilgrim.'

A couple of nights later in Pendueles, the owner of the hostel where I stayed offered to wash my clothes and cook us all dinner. He showed us, a little group of strangers with whom he would share his life and home for just one evening, the most incredible kindness. In the morning as I was leaving, even though he spoke very little English, and me even less Spanish, I asked him where this kindness came from. And it was almost as if he didn't understand the question. For he was a follower of Jesus, he said. He was a pilgrim himself. He was someone whose life was rooted in and shaped by the things we see and learn from Jesus. He was someone who said the Lord's Prayer each day. He said that his life now was to help others.

9

FORGIVE US OUR SINS

For years, I was a bit of a snob when it came to reading. I would only read what I considered to be 'proper fiction'. I had read one or two crime novels, Agatha Christie and the like, but usually I would settle down with something I considered more highbrow, and probably on the Booker shortlist. Then, about ten years ago, my brother-in-law, who reads an awful lot of crime fiction, challenged me. In fact, he may well have called me a bit of a snob who looked down my nose at people like him and the books they were reading but had never really given them a try. So I asked him to recommend me something.

Now, he is a fan of American crime fiction, so he lent me a copy of a Robert B. Parker novel and then suggested I move on to Michael Connelly.

I was hooked. I still read other books as well, but now I almost always have a crime novel of one sort or another on the go. I love them. And so do many other people. But why?

Last year I met Ian Rankin, the very popular bestselling Scottish crime writer, and we chatted about this very subject. He quickly gave me the answer. It is partly because they are just very good stories, and usually ones with a clear beginning, middle and end, but it is mostly because they are about good and evil, the reality of human failing and human sinfulness and how we contend with it.

Their subject matter is darkness. The darkness in the human heart and where it leads us. And usually how even those who battle against the darkness, like his flawed but compelling hero, the detective Rebus, can't really pretend that it is ever possible to be free of it, or to imagine that we too aren't capable of committing the very crimes we abhor in others.

This is what the Church calls sin. On the one hand, it is not a very popular concept nowadays, most of us preferring to be understood rather than forgiven. On the other, sin is all too real, and very well recognised, even if we use other words to describe it. Hence the popularity of crime novels.

Let me give just one obvious and almost universal experience of how each of us is aware of our own sinfulness.

So, imagine you are lying in bed tonight. Or tomorrow night. Or yesterday. Or any night, for that matter!

You sift through the events of the day. You review what's happened: what you said, what you did, what you *didn't* do. And you berate yourself. Why did I say that? Why did I do the other? Or sometimes it's the things we don't do that haunt us. Why *didn't* I say that? Why *didn't* I do the other? Why did I miss that opportunity? Why was I so slow to offer help? That colleague needed support. My daughter needed my time. And so on.

Is there anyone who has not had this experience? If there is, I've not met them.

Paul put it very succinctly when he commented in bitter desperation that this was his experience as well. 'I do not understand what I do,' he said. 'For what I want to do I do not do, but what I hate I do' (Romans 7:15, NIV).

Isn't this the lot of all of us? We look back over the day, and we look back over our lives, and we chastise ourselves, or even condemn ourselves, for the things we failed to do, the terrible things we said, the kind and generous things we failed to do, the affirming words we never got round to saying.

Regrets and despair take hold of our heart. Some people even end up hating themselves.

All of this is, sadly, quite normal.

When we find ourselves thinking this way, what is actually happening is this: we soberly appraise ourselves and conclude that we have fallen short of our own standards. We are not the people we want to be, and not the people we aspire to be. We are less than we intend to be, and less than we want ourselves to be.

This is sin. There is a lot more that could be said, but it isn't a bad place to start, because this very beautiful and challenging petition in the Lord's Prayer makes no sense unless we have some understanding of sin; that is, *the wilful choosing of what we know to be wrong and the wilful neglect of what we know to be right.*

We're not talking about mistakes. We're not talking about failure. It's quite possible to set out to do the right thing, and for all sorts of reasons it doesn't happen. This is different.

And we're not talking about the vagaries of different personality preferences, where some behaviours come natur-ally to some people and not to others. We're not saying that it's all somebody else's fault, and that if we had been brought up differently, given different opportunities, been dealt a different hand in life, then we would behave differently.

No, it is to look ourselves in the mirror and simply observe that we are not the people we want to be. We fall short of our own standards. We choose what is wrong. We neglect what is right.

To understand the depth and importance of this petition in the Lord's Prayer, we must start here. We need to recover what sin means before we are able to find forgiveness. In our society, the whole concept of sin has become outmoded. For some, it is even repugnant. They think it means adhering to an impossibly difficult and 'beyond our reach' set of external standards, rather than the inner call of the compass of our own conscience, the standards we set for ourselves. But what I'm saying is that the inner call of our conscience is actually a very good place to start, because we all have this in-built sense of right and wrong, and we all fall short. We may say, 'If it feels good, do it,' but many of us privately admit that we did something because it seemed attractive and good, but in so doing we hurt others and therefore hurt ourselves as well. Just because no one else sees it, doesn't mean it isn't real, or make its impact any less devastating.

Moreover, other people might hear the bad things I say, but may never notice the good things I fail to say, still less the grudges, petty hatreds, jealousies that swarm my mind.

Therefore, if we start with our own estimations of ourselves, then at least we have a common currency, and can begin to understand why the Christian faith speaks about *everyone* being a sinner, and *all* of us falling short. Suddenly, it becomes quite an ordinary thing to say, because it is precisely what each one of us says about ourselves.

Of course, we also need to understand ourselves, and the reasons behind our failings and the muddled motives that subconsciously direct us. Some of us fail to affirm others because we never received affirmation ourselves and don't know how to do it. Others who have been wounded and abused and shamelessly let down by life will sometimes end up wounding others. Though none of this is inevitable. There are always choices to make. But counselling and therapy will help us understand ourselves. They are part of the way God helps us to heal and helps us to grow and be forgiven. Saying we have sinned and need forgiveness doesn't prevent us from also being wounded and needing to be healed, and the two things are not the same.

The unending goodness and forgiveness of God

We human beings are a complex totality of mind, body and spirit. There are all sorts of things, some of them locked deeply in early childhood experiences, which shape the people we become, and continue to shape and influence our decisions and actions. Understanding more about this is a good thing. It may even go a long way towards helping us understand ourselves, right down to why we say the things we say and do the things we do. But I'm not sure that for any of us it can ever entirely explain why we still often choose to act selfishly, or withhold things from others, or even find ourselves taking some petty delight in someone else's disappointment or downfall. In fact, the more I understand myself, even though it is extremely helpful in enabling me to grow and take responsibility, the more I am brought closer to a much harder conclusion; that I am never going to be completely the person I want to be, and there is no use blaming this on others, or on the circumstances of my upbringing, or on other things that stymied me or got in my way.

In other words, there is still that place where each of us knows that we choose to do what we know to be wrong.

That we avoid doing what is right. That we put ourselves first.

And – just to raise the bar higher! – on top of this, the Christian faith tells us that there are external standards as well. Standards beyond even those we set ourselves.

These standards are demonstrated in the astonishing actions and teachings of Jesus Christ, someone who doesn't just choose not to take revenge on those who hurt him, but having been slapped on one cheek offers his attacker the other; someone who having been robbed of his jacket offers his coat as well (Matthew 5:38–40). He doesn't just *say* that we should love our enemies and forgive those who hurt us; we see him *do* it. On the cross, he even offers forgiveness to the soldiers who nail him there. He reaches out in love to the thieves crucified alongside him.

The standard set by Jesus is very, very challenging. It means living out the beatitudes that we looked at in a previous chapter: living as a child of God's kingdom, taking seriously what it means to say to God, 'Your will be done in my life as I see it in Jesus.' Therefore, to live life as I see Jesus live life does not mean adhering to a ridiculously naive, alien and external set of mean-spirited restrictions on my liberty, but to live a glorious and beautiful 'fully alive' life. For what I see in Jesus is someone who is perfectly human, without regret or failure, tempted as I am in every way (because he is completely human as I am completely human), and yet able to rise above the negative forces that drag us down or push us sideways. And what I hear Jesus say and what I see in his life is something I want for my life. In him, there is an authenticity I can never quite attain, but will spend my life reaching for.

This is a way of inhabiting life that is far above the

observation of rules, way beyond just a moral code to follow. It is a way of love. It shows me that I don't only fall short of my own standards, I fall short of God's standards as well. And even if I do keep all the Commandments and all the rules (as I should and as I try!) I will never be able to love like Jesus, and I will probably always end up putting myself first.

Which really should be very depressing and a recipe for more sleepless nights as I compare myself to Christ and realise what a schmuck I am.

Only it isn't.

I may beat myself up over my behaviour. But God doesn't.

God offers forgiveness. This is why Jesus has come into the world. To shows us how to be human and to restore us to relationship with God – and to forgive sins.

It is all there in what is probably the most famous verse in the Bible, that 'God so loved the world that he gave his only Son, so that everyone who believes in him may not perish but may have eternal life' (John 3:16). In Jesus, God is saving the world from itself, and from the fact that we humans fail.

Which is why I must pray, 'Forgive us our trespasses.'

I turn to Christ, as did that thief upon the cross.

I reach out to God so that I might receive God's merciful love and endlessly restorative forgiveness.

God won't force me to do this. God *calls* me to repent. But God won't *make* me repent. This is because, having been made in the image of God, we are made in the image of one who is completely free, and therefore we have this wonderful, dangerous freedom ourselves. We are free to turn to God *and* free to turn away.

God isn't playing tricks on us. We have this freedom for a reason. It is love. As I have written about elsewhere, for love to be real it has to be free. God could have done it differently.

We could live in a universe where everything worked like clockwork and all the creatures in it were pre-programmed to do only what is right. There would be no meddlesome freedom. But in such a universe there would be good order and there would be good behaviour, there would be complete obedience, but there wouldn't be love. If we have no choice, we have no possibility of love. For to love someone is to choose to put them first. To make decisions that are not necessarily in your own best interest. To give yourself to someone in a way that is beyond obedience and defies logic. No one can be forced to love.

Therefore, in the universe we *do* have, God takes the great risk of creating a creature that is capable of love. And for that creature to exist, there must also be the freedom *not* to love, to be selfish and hateful, even to end up never loving God and never saying sorry; and despite all the evidence of God's creative purposes in the world, free to choose *not* to know God, and to reject others. Which is why God also takes the risk of sending Jesus into the world in a way that had to be ambiguous. God had to preserve our freedom to choose. Like God, Jesus shows us what love looks like, offers the medicine of forgiveness, but leaves us to decide whether we will accept it or not. Which is the decision we have to make every time we say the Lord's Prayer. Am I sorry for my sins? Do I want to be forgiven? Am I trying to live differently?

If we are able to say yes, however tentatively, then, para-doxically, in a culture which has eschewed all this stupid talk of sinfulness we are able to say, 'Come back sin, all is forgiven.'

We may be miserable about our sins, but we don't need to be miserable sinners. As St Augustine observed, we were 'washed once in the waters of baptism and we are washed daily when asking for forgiveness in the Lord's Prayer'.[1] It is part of the daily discipline of a Christian life.

Moreover, God offers the great abundant blessing of forgiveness freely and immediately. God is much more ready to forgive than we are to repent. God is like the loving father of the prodigal son, who seeing him on the horizon runs out to embrace him. God is the loving mother who gathers her children around her.

Better still, not only does God forgive, God also forgets. God doesn't even remember our transgressions (see Isaiah 43:25; Hebrews 8:12). We may continue to punish ourselves over our failings – and in this life we will have to live with their consequences – but in heaven, God has washed our sins away.

This is how it is with love. This is how a parent loves and forgives a child. God endlessly offers this forgiveness, but we need to turn to God to receive it. We need to respond with sorrow and penitence for what we have done wrong. We need to face up to and accept the consequences in this life. We need to be ready to forgive others.

IO.

AS WE FORGIVE THOSE WHO SIN AGAINST US

With our astonishing freedom to love and to be loved comes the great likelihood we will get things wrong. This, we conclude, is the human condition. It is there from the very beginning. The serpent tempts Eve. She tricks Adam. He blames her. She blames the snake. They end up trying to hide from God.

So it goes on, even down to each of us. There is a solidarity in our sinfulness, and there is, therefore, a solidarity in our need of God. And God, in God's great goodness, has sent us the remedy: Jesus himself, and him crucified. For just as this single line in the Lord's Prayer goes on to say that we should 'forgive those who trespass against us', and just as God does indeed forgive us, we come to realise that all our failings and shortcomings are a trespass against God, because they mean we are not living in the way that is best for us, nor the way that God intends. Therefore, as we are forgiven by God, so we too should forgive others.

This isn't as easy or as straightforward as it may first appear. Even though we may be able to agree that there is something called sin. And we may agree it has a grip in every life and that we need forgiveness. And even though we can

107

probably find it quite easy to agree that this forgiveness is a wonderful gift (and that God gives it to us with a glorious, profligate freedom, not because we deserve it or can earn it, but because of God's great love for us), we are not necessarily so sure about forgiving others.

At this point, the Lord's Prayer starts to feel very uncomfortable. As we reflect on this petition, we start to realise that the forgiveness we long for for ourselves comes with a condition. We must forgive others too.

The New Testament is insistent about this. 'Forgive, and you will be forgiven,' says Jesus (Luke 6:37). 'Just as the Lord has forgiven you, so you also must forgive,' says Paul (Colossians 3:13). 'How often should I forgive? As many as seven times?' asks Peter. No, says Jesus, 'seventy-seven times' (Matthew 18:21–22).

Moreover, this teaching might even have a rather uncomfortable sting in the tail. We ask God to forgive us *as we forgive those who sin against us.*

Is this really what I want? Do I want God to forgive me in the same way that I forgive others?

Actually, this is the last thing I want. I know how very unforgiving I am. I know how I foster grudges against others. I know that what I really want is revenge upon those who have wronged me. I long for their downfall, not their forgiveness.

The painful challenge of these words is that if I want the beautiful 'without conditions forgiveness' that God offers me in Jesus Christ, I must take hold of the *one* condition outlined here, which is to offer the same to others.

I am not very good at this. I try to give the outward impression of someone who is generous and forgiving. But inside, my heart is still hard. Paradoxically, what I need more than anything is the generous blessing of God's forgiveness to melt my heart. And I may best find this by starting to practise it on others.

But then I face another challenge. What if those I am called to forgive don't want to be forgiven? What if they throw it back at me? What if they fail to show any penitence or remorse? I understand and I'm very grateful that Jesus died for me while I was still a sinner. I understand that the forgiveness he offers is not dependent upon my penitence, but nevertheless I should be sorry. In fact, perhaps my greatest sin is my lack of sorrow for my sins.

So how am I supposed to approach the person who has wronged me and hurt me, but who shows no penitence at all, who delights in my downfall and who laughs in my face? And what does it mean for people who have been far more badly hurt than I have?

Are parents of murdered children supposed to forgive their children's killers? Are those who have been abused supposed to forgive their abuser?

I am fortunate enough to have never faced such horror or abuse, so I am not going to sit in judgement on those who find it impossible to forgive. Nor am I able to say that forgiveness is cheap. It cost God the life of Jesus on the cross. It requires penitence. But what I see in Jesus is one who goes on forgiving, even forgiving those who betray him, abuse him and nail him to the cross. It doesn't mean there are no consequences for those who have perpetrated such horrors. Perhaps, for us, it therefore means being *ready* to forgive and not letting hatred or a desire for revenge take hold in our hearts, because in the end we will be the ones who suffer. Our souls will be in danger.

Moreover, as Stephen Cherry points out, sometimes there is 'grace in not forgiving' – or in not forgiving yet – 'but in retaining a non-hateful, non-vengeful indignation, and acting on a righteous and responsible desire to name the wrong and call to account those who have abused their power. This is the grace of honesty and patience. Sometimes the grace of forgiving will have to wait until truth and justice have had their day.'[1]

A change of heart

I don't want a hard heart. I don't want bitterness and cynicism to take root in my heart. I don't want to be governed by regret, failure and a desire for revenge. I want a heart like Jesus' heart, one that is ready and able to forgive, but also one that laments over human failure and one that hungers and thirsts for what is right, and, therefore, also one that breaks.

However, sometimes appearing too quick to forgive enables those who have perpetrated terrible injustices to avoid the just consequences of their actions and further punishes those who have been oppressed by them. Therefore, being *ready* to forgive but waiting for repentance and working for justice is the way we best witness to the command of Jesus that we all be reconciled to God and work for the outworking of God's will.

All this is enormously difficult. I know there is sin in the world. I know there is sin in my own heart. I know I want and need to be forgiven. But I also know that I must forgive others. But unless and until there is a culture in our world whose hallmark is forgiveness, then revenge and further conflict will continue to rise up.

So, I take great solace in the fact that this is a prayer. I am addressing these words to God. I am saying to the God who

110

is the Prince of Peace, the one whose character is revealed to me in Jesus, that I want to be forgiven, that I want to be made whole, that I want to live in a world whose currency is love, and I am praying for the grace and strength to be able to forgive.

Classically, when it comes to forgiveness this is why the Church has always taught there must be penitence, and, after absolution and forgiveness, there must be amendment of life. We need to hold these things together – the readiness to forgive alongside the readiness to repent and the determination to change, even if we know we will probably fall again.

Finally, I take even greater solace from the knowledge that God is the judge of these things, not me. Even when I find I'm unable to forgive, when the wrongs I have received cut so deep and I just don't have forgiveness to offer, I pray that God will save my heart from hardening, so I am at least able to *contemplate* forgiveness were this person one day to express their penitence. And that God may have mercy on me.

Does the fact that the version of the Lord's Prayer that I read in Matthew's Gospel uses the word 'debt' rather than 'sin' change any of this? Well, not really. It may even raise the bar another notch, for the debt I owe is not just due to my individual sins, but to the wider collective failings of a society which takes for granted discrepancies of wealth, unremitting poverty for some and obscene wealth for others, the degradation of the environment and conflict after conflict, greed upon greed. Moreover, language changes. In the same way that the word 'trespass' used to mean more than straying onto someone else's property, so the word 'debt' used to mean more than a financial debt.

These other words help us understand that sin is not just

about crossing a line but about missing a mark. There are things we do which are wrong. But there are also things we don't do which could have been good.

What is not in doubt is the fact that sin is bigger than my individual sins, dark and ghastly though they be. Paul in his letter to the church in Rome speaks about sin as if it is an 'oppressive power that squats on humanity'.[2] He speaks, for instance, of 'another law at war with the law of my mind, making me captive to the law of sin' (Romans 7:23). He says that 'all have sinned and fall short of the glory of God' (Romans 3:23). Therefore, we acknowledge the web of sin which ensnares us all, even beyond our own direct responsibility and awareness.

The Christian faith teaches us this. It enables us to cry out for the sin of all the world. And for our own sins. It shows us where the boundaries are. But it also encourages us to transcend those boundaries, and, like Jesus, to strive for those things which are hard to measure, but which we know to be the most important and the most beautiful, like kindness and compassion, generosity and gentleness.

This is the big debt we owe.

We haven't done something wrong if we decide *not* to be kind to someone. We *have* done something wrong if we choose deliberately to be unkind to them.

But if we withhold the possibility of kindness, then we are living lives that are less than the beautiful, fully human life we see in Jesus.

Sin, therefore, is complex. It is, *simply*, the things we choose to do wrong. But it is also, *complicatedly*, all the things we could and should do if we were less self-centred and more like Jesus. And *collectively* it is the sins of the whole world, in all its misery and conflict.

Spiritual exercise

Think of saying the Lord's Prayer each day as a spiritual exercise. Just as going to the gym for a workout, doing fifty press ups, or even taking the dog for a walk, will train our body, so the recitation of the words that Jesus gives us trains our soul. It helps us get to the heart of things. It helps us understand ourselves better. The heart of Jesus beats in us. We see both the simplicity and the complexity of sin. We cry out to God for our own sins to be forgiven, but we also cultivate habits of generous forgiveness to others, so that we are ready to forgive those who hurt us, and, even in those circumstances where that is thrown back in our face, or when people's abject lack of repentance and determination to go on hurting makes forgiveness impossible, our own soul is not stained by bitterness, anger, or a desire for revenge. Our hearts continue to reflect and bear witness to the heart of Christ. We begin to become people who can change things. We bear witness to what the world could be if it followed Christ, if it repented of its sin.

And knowing we need to be forgiven, we are able to forgive others and be ready to forgive those who, we pray, will come to repentance one day.

In the end, we know that only God can forgive. And we know that Jesus forgives because he is the perfect expression of God's love, but also because, on the cross, he became the victim and took upon himself the sins of the world.

We are called to be forgiving. 'Blessed are the merciful,' says Jesus, 'for they will receive mercy' (Matthew 5:7).

But we are called to carry on being ready to forgive even when we receive no mercy. Let me conclude this chapter with an inspiring story of what this looks like in action.

During the Second World War, Leonard Wilson, Bishop of Singapore and later Bishop of Birmingham, was interned by the Japanese and tortured in the camp at Changi.

Preaching about his experience in 1946 and what it taught him about following Jesus, he recalled words of one of my predecessors, Archbishop William Temple.

Temple had written that if we pray for a particular virtue, whether it be patience or courage or love, one of the ways that God answers this is by giving us opportunity to express it.

This is not, perhaps, the answer to prayer we would choose, and Wilson said this in his sermon:

After my first beating I was almost afraid to pray for courage lest I should have another opportunity of exercising it; but my unspoken prayer was there, and without God's help I doubt whether I should have come through.

Long hours of ignoble pain were a severe test. In the middle of that torture, they asked me if I still believed in God. When by God's help I said, 'I do', they asked me why God did not save me; and by the help of his Holy Spirit I said, 'God does save me. He does not save me by freeing me from pain or punishment, but he saves me by giving me the spirit to bear it.' And when they asked me why I did not curse them, I told them it was because I was a follower of Jesus Christ, who taught us that we were all brethren.

I did not like to use the words, 'Father, forgive them.' It seemed too blasphemous to use our Lord's words, but I felt them, and I said 'Father, I know these men are doing their duty. Help them to see that I am innocent.' And when I muttered 'Forgive them,' I wondered how far I was being dramatic, and if I really meant it, because I looked at their faces as they stood round and took it in turn to flog, and their faces were hard and cruel, and some of them were evidently enjoying their cruelty.

But by the grace of God, I saw those men not as they were, but as they had been. Once they were little children playing with their brothers and sisters and happy in their parents' love . . . and it is hard to hate little children. But even that was not enough. Then came into my mind as I lay on the table the words of that communion hymn:

> Look, Father, look on his anointed face,
> and only look on us as found in him.

And so, I saw them, not as they were, not as they had been, but as they were capable of becoming, redeemed by the power of Christ; and I knew that it was only common sense to say 'forgive'.[3]

Few of us will, thank God, find ourselves tested in this way.

But this is the way of Christ. To see ourselves and others as God sees us and loves us. And to be found in Christ. And to forgive, as he forgives.

It is also the only hope for our world.

And the alternative is on show each day in the terrible inequalities and depravities of our world, which means that even in a country like the UK, the sixth wealthiest in the world, child poverty continues to rise and asylum seekers fleeing terror and torture are treated with indignity; where Christians in Gaza and the West Bank are not able to worship today as we are, where war foments and conflict smoulders – in the Holy Land itself, in Ukraine, Yemen and Sudan, in human hearts bent on endless retribution, unfound by grace, endlessly banging the table for what we have decided is just, but with no mercy whatsoever.

This is the world without Christ, without his teaching, without his prayer, where he reaches out to our sorrows and pleads with us to think again, but we do not listen, so conditioned by vengeful hatefulness and all that has proceeded from it that we do not hear him calling our name, do not see him standing among us.

After eight months, and the most unimaginably awful torture, Bishop Wilson was released. He wrote about the joy of seeing sunlight again. He said it was like a foretaste of resurrection and that of course God is to be found on the cross, sharing in the sufferings of the world, but it is the resurrection that has the final word.

One last amazing thing.

After the end of the Second World War and when Singapore was liberated, some of the men who had tortured Bishop Wilson came back to find him. They asked him to baptise them. This is the power of forgiveness.

II.

LEAD US NOT INTO TEMPTATION, BUT DELIVER US FROM EVIL

We are back where we started. Life is hard and dangerous. The way forward isn't obvious. There are many distractions and temptations. There is evil as well as good. Jesus, please be our guide. We can't do this on our own.

I've been writing this bit of the book while staying at St Hilda's Priory in Whitby, the home of the wonderfully named Order of the Holy Paraclete. 'Paraclete' is the untranslatable-into-English Greek word that Jesus uses in John's Gospel for the Spirit (see, for example, John 15:26). The one who shows us the way.

Having been happily writing all day (for me this is a happy place: the stillness, prayer and hospitality of the sisters and a space away from the diary to think and write) and with the afternoon winding to a close, I have decided to go for a walk. Down the hill into Whitby itself.

It is late October. Drizzly. The nights are drawing in. The clocks go back at the weekend.

Whitby is still lovely.

Huge waves crash against the cliffs and splash across the

harbour wall. But inside the harbour the water is calm and either side of the mouth of the River Esk, the town spreads itself out and climbs up the hill. Beyond me, on the other side of the harbour, is the imposing ruin of the abbey where Hilda herself ministered and where important bits of English church history unfolded.

This part of the Yorkshire coast is strikingly beautiful. From Ripon, York and Lastingham, from Rievaulx and Fountains, up the coast to Jarrow and Monkwearmouth, Hexham and Durham and to Holy Island itself, the saints, like Hilda and Cuthbert, Paulinus, Wilfrid, Caedmon, Bede and Cedd, whose feast day is today, the day I'm writing, still make their presence felt. They are human cairns on the spiritual landscape showing us we're going the right way. They are people who were led by the Spirit and whose lives were shaped by prayer – this prayer, the prayer the Lord taught, the prayer he wants to teach us today. And the places that are associated with them, and many other places, indeed wherever two or three are gathered together in the name of Jesus and utter the prayer of Jesus; these places are hallowed.

This is good air to breathe. These are good paths to follow.

I wander around the town. I do a bit of window shopping. I get something to eat. Fish and chips, of course, at the famous Magpie Café. Is there anywhere better?

Leaving the café, it's getting dark. I turn to go back to the priory, but not for the first time in my life, I'm unsure of the way. Some people are born with an inner satnav. Not me.

I know it's uphill. (That bit is easy!) And I know I need to stay on the north side of the river. (I'm not that useless!) But I'm not really sure which road to take.

Coming down the hill earlier, I was in a bit of a dream.

Thinking about the book and enjoying the views of the sea, I meandered, knowing that sooner or later I would hit the harbour and get my bearings. For the return journey, however, I need to be a bit more precise.

Following an instinct (rarely a good thing to do in these situations) I set off up one of the roads leading out of the town in what I think is roughly the right direction. After about a mile, I realise it isn't.

Of course, I should have got my phone out earlier and consulted the satnav that has been in my pocket the whole time. But I'm not in a hurry, so it doesn't really matter that I've taken the scenic route. With Google Maps I'm able to correct myself. I'm pointed back onto the right path.

The inner satnav of grace

The Lord's Prayer ends with the petition 'lead us not into temptation'. Our immediate response might be that, despite the impressive brevity of the prayer, this is actually one petition too many. Surely, it is surplus to requirements: God would never *lead us* into temptation. We hardly need to ask God not to do something God would never even consider in the first place.

So why is it here?

It's because we get lost. Because we are led into temptation. Because we struggle. Because we often lead *ourselves* into temptation.

We get seduced and ensnared by things we know to be wrong, and because we often do the things we don't want to do, and wander from the path, trusting ourselves, seeking our own kingdoms.

So, this petition means that, when I am tempted, when I confront what I know to be wrong, even evil itself, I am saying, 'Lord, be with me, hold me and help me and be my guide. Your presence, and this prayer you give me, are the inner compass, the inner satnav, which will save me and always put me back on the right path.'

'It is,' says Stephen Cherry, 'a prayer of self-awareness from those who have come to appreciate that they may not be able to face or manage or cope with everything the future brings.'[1]

And evil is real. Jesus was tempted. He was tempted by the devil at the beginning of his ministry. Tempted in the Garden of Gethsemane. And he confronted evil. Judas betrayed him. His friends abandoned him. The religious and political leaders of the day seized him. They dressed him up as a king and mocked him. They brought false charges against him. The mob bayed for his blood. They enjoyed the spectacle of his death. Weak leaders washed their hands of him. Religious leaders thought it expedient that he was eliminated. The crowds who watched him die made fun of him. The soldiers who nailed him to the tree rolled dice for his clothes. Outside the city walls, where other decaying corpses festered and where the rubbish heap of Sheol smouldered, the forces of darkness caught up with him. He was crucified between two criminals. It was all over in a few hours.

There was darkness over the land, and it seemed as if the darkness had triumphed.

But what appeared to be the most colossal and decisive defeat was actually a victory. As the soldiers come to break the legs of the crucified men to hasten their dying, they find that Jesus is already dead. Just to make sure, they pierce his heart with a lance. John tells us that blood and water flowed from his broken heart. Signs of life and hope, baptism and Eucharist, flowing from the cross, a river of life (see John 19:31–34).

His body is sealed in a tomb and, fearful that his followers might steal his body away, a guard is appointed.

Night falls, and then a second day, and another night, and on the third day, while it is still dark, and very early in the morning, Mary Magdalene comes to the tomb and finds it empty, the stone rolled away.

She fetches Peter and John, but they don't really know what is happening. As they rush away, Mary lingers at the tomb.

Mary is standing in the dawning brightness of the first day of the new creation.

She is aware of a presence with her. She turns and sees Jesus. She beholds, as it were, the first piece of the new creation, the risen Christ, but she doesn't recognise him.

He speaks to her. 'Why are you weeping?' he says. 'For whom are you looking?' (John 20:15) These are very beautiful questions. I've written about them elsewhere.[2] Jesus rises from the dead, and his first thoughts are for our welfare. He longs to wipe away the tears from our eyes. He wants to make sure we go in the right direction, and he is challenging us to decide who it is we're going to follow.

Mary, still not recognising him, says that she's looking for Jesus and if he, the gardener whom she assumes him to be, knows what they have done with his body, could he tell her?

Then Jesus speaks her name, and as she hears her name spoken her eyes are opened. She recognises him. '*Rabbouni*,' she says, which means 'Teacher' (John 20:16). She calls him Rabbi. The one who guides us. The one who teaches us. The one who shows us the way, even through death itself.

Naturally enough, she clings on to him. But Jesus, gently releasing himself from her grip, says, 'Do not hold on to me . . . But go to my brothers and say to them, "I am ascending to my Father and your Father, to my God and your God"' (John 20:17). Which says to me there is *always more*. You never stop learning how to follow Jesus, and you never get to the end of prayer, because prayer *is* love and has no ending – and it is *always ours*, never mine alone.

Here is the liberating good news of the Christian faith. We do not need to face evil and death. Jesus has done it for us.

There is still evil in the world, and one day, we will all die. But we face these trials, even find ourselves sharing in the suffering of Christ, knowing that Jesus has saved us and has already won the victory over darkness, sin and death.

This victory is for all of us; for every person. And we must share it with everyone. Even those who seem farthest away and least interested. This is why in the Apostles' Creed that is said in the Anglican Church every day during Evensong there is a petition saying that 'he descended into hell'.[3] Jesus' confrontation with darkness and evil plumbs the very depths of darkness and despair, even the depths of hell itself. The beautiful music of the gospel, the song of the resurrection, is there for everyone, drawing us in. We must share it in the same beautiful, generous, non-coercive way we see in Jesus. It is an invitation. And we have the freedom to ignore it.

Which is, tragically, precisely what happens. Many take no notice. As we do ourselves from time to time. Which is why we need to go on being penitent.

Sometimes we even face the temptation that we may throw away the greatest gift of all, that even though we know these very beautiful things, we will choose to reject them, forget them, ignore them. We will go our own way. We will trespass and fail. The shiny and temporal seductions of the world will lead us astray.

'Save us in the time of trial,' says the Lord's Prayer. It is another way of saying 'Lead us not into temptation', and this phrase appears in some versions of the prayer. We are asking that in those moments of wilful neglect and great temptation, we will be led back to the beauty of the gospel, that we will hear Jesus saying to us, as he said to his disciples on the night before he died, 'I am going now to prepare a place for you. And after I have gone, I shall return to take you with me' (John 14:3, *paraphrased*). Our immersion in the prayer of Jesus, and our very particular daily recitation of this prayer, will be our compass.

In the cross and resurrection, Jesus meets us at the point of our deepest need, the place of the most profound human failing: the murder of an innocent man. In his death, Jesus stands alongside all those other countless thousands and millions of innocent deaths and grotesque human failings, and he leads us home.

It is where the Lord's Prayer ends. With a profound realism about human profanity, waywardness and failing; and with the everlasting beauty of the cross, though this time the crosses that we hold are bursting into life. There is an ancient tradition of depicting the cross that sometimes shows it coming to life blossoming and flowering from the very places where Jesus' feet were nailed, his heart was pierced and his head crowned with thorns.

'To pray "deliver us from evil" is to inhale the victory of the Cross,' says Tom Wright.[4] 'We wade to that land of peace through a sea of war,' notes Crossan.[5] Storms rage around us. Snares lie at our feet. Siren voices tempt us to stray. Cynics scoff. But we are safe in Jesus. And even when we walk into the darkness of death itself, we find it belongs to God.

'Even though I walk through the darkest valley, I fear no evil; for you are with me; your rod and your staff – they comfort me' (Psalm 23:4). These very famous words from Psalm 23 offer the reassurance that God is with us – even in times of trial, even in darkness, even in death itself. We make them our own as we say 'lead us not into temptation'.

Our hearts are fortified by God's heart. We find our home there.

Part Four

FOR THE KINGDOM, THE POWER AND THE GLORY ARE YOURS, NOW AND FOR EVER

Every prayer should be brought to its conclusion with the glorification of God through Christ in the Holy Spirit.

ORIGEN[1]

We finish with what is called a doxology. The Greek word *doxo* means 'praise'. We draw the prayer together in thanks and praise of God, and in this doxology, we reassert our conviction that everything that matters belongs to God and comes from God.

You won't find this bit in either Matthew or Luke's version of the Lord's Prayer, though there are ancient versions of the Bible where it does appear. The theory is that because this is the way we say it in church (and this is how it appears in the most ancient Christian document outside of the Bible, the *Didache*) then it naturally got added in. But most scholars agree that this is an ending we have added on because it is similar to the way many prayers conclude.

Finally, we say 'Amen', which means 'I agree'. We put a personal stamp of endorsement on a prayer we have said together.

12

KINGDOM, POWER AND GLORY FOR EVER

Rule, agency, magnificence: these belong to God for ever.

We have already spoken about God's kingdom and what it means. And why God's name is hallowed and glorious.

But what about power? What do we mean when we say that God is powerful?

We usually understand power to be the ability to influence and shape people and events. But there are different types of power.[1] A teacher or a high court judge is powerful because of the position they hold. A brain surgeon or a plumber is powerful because of the skills they possess. Others are powerful because of their ability to communicate ideas and influence others. We all have power of one kind or another.

But we don't all have authority. Authority isn't quite the same as power. Writer and thinker John Kotter has said that 'power is the ability to influence others to get things done, while authority is the formal rights that come to a person who occupies a particular position, since power does not necessarily accompany a position'.[2]

So a social media influencer has a lot of power. The power to influence people, their behaviour and their actions. But not much authority. They can't *make* people do things.

A police officer has authority. If they tell you to slow down on the motorway, you must obey. If you don't, you will get a speeding ticket. But it may not influence you that much. It is a different sort of power. Next time you are on the motorway you may choose to speed again.

God has power *and* authority. God is the one to whom we are all ultimately accountable. God is the source and origin of everything. God chooses to exercise that power in ways that influence us and shape us, thus always preserving our freedom to choose how we respond, but God's ultimate authority and our ultimate accountability remain in place.

Writing about the incarnation, David Gitari, one of the great bishops of the East African Anglican Church, has written that Jesus, as the incarnate Word of God, reveals Christ's divinity 'not so much in mighty acts, though these were important, but in the revelation of divine glory through loving and humble service'.[3] He goes on: 'the essence of Christian revelation is that God has now spoken in his Son because Jesus Christ perfectly shows all that is knowable about the Father.'[4] In Christ, the incarnate Word, God tells his story in the only language we understand, the language of another human life. This life reveals perfectly what God is like; to have seen Jesus is to have seen the Father.[5] It is the story of Christ that leads us to the source of power, which is the love of God.

Christ, therefore, possesses formal and positional power as the Son of God, the incarnate Word. This also gives him reputational and instrumental power. However, one of the earliest descriptions of the person of Christ in Scripture uses the language of *kenosis* (a Greek word that is usually translated as 'emptying') rather than power; what Sarah Coakley calls 'power-in-vulnerability'.[6] The famous biblical passage is from Paul's letter to the Philippians where it says, 'though

130

he was in the form of God, [Jesus] did not regard equality with God as something to be exploited, but emptied himself, taking the form of a slave' (Philippians 2:6–7).

However, exactly what the word *kenosis* means isn't entirely clear. It is only used once in Scripture, in this passage, and its meaning is disputed. It is usually assumed that Christ is laying aside the power that he possesses as the second person of the Trinity. But what if this *kenosis* is not the temporary emptying out of power, but the revelation of a different sort of power which is now emptied into humanity, re-shaping our entire understanding of power and authority?

In the same way we can acknowledge that Christ possessed great power of communication and skill. He built around him a strong coalition of like-minded followers. He was able to apply sanctions if he needed to. Yet, he chooses to be silent before those who conspire against him.[7] Almost all who follow him abandon him.[8] Even though he had extraordinary powers to heal the sick and raise the dead (he is the one of whom people said, 'Even the winds and the sea obey him'[9]). When faced with his own trial and execution and the terrifying hold of the powers that rage against him, he refuses to use the power he has.[10]

This is not to say that Christ never deploys his power – far from it. But if the ultimate revelation of God in Christ is found in his passion, death and resurrection (and if this is his supreme act of 'leadership', the means whereby we are reconciled to God), then looking at how Christ exercises power *in his passion and death* will give us the clearest insight into what it means to say 'Thine is the kingdom, the power and the glory', and help us grasp how a Christian understanding of power, influence and leadership can be exercised in our world today.

The power of authenticity

On the cross, more than anywhere else, Jesus is demonstrating what God's power is actually like. Our human categories of power, those that come from position, ability, reputation, education and training, are limited and provisional. They shrink back when they see the power of love. They cannot describe the power we see in Christ. For when we consider Christ's *actual* power, the power of Christ lifted up, and his glory and power on the cross, we immediately notice two other things that are distinctive and emblematic of the power of God *emptied into* Christ.

First, there is what I am going to call *the power of authenticity*.

Right at the end of the Sermon on the Mount in Matthew chapters 5–7, when Jesus finishes speaking, the crowds are amazed at his teaching, 'for he taught them as one having authority, and not as their scribes' (Matthew 7:29). Although the crowds use the word 'authority', and in the context of Matthew's Gospel their assessment is based upon the entire sermon which 'the reader can now judge for himself',[11] I believe this is best understood as referring to Jesus' authenticity. What is different about Jesus' teaching is not just the content, but the fact that what he says aligns with who he is. So, for instance, the difficult teaching about going the second mile[12] and loving your enemies and praying for those who persecute you[13] is lived out in the whole of Jesus' ministry and especially in his passion and death. James Lawrence persuasively argues that it is this authenticity, this alignment between what is said and what is done, between the narrative and the life lived, that made Jesus so attractive and drew people to him.[14] Authenticity is the heart of effective leadership and one of the greatest sources of a power which liberates and heals.

The power of undefended love

The second distinctive feature of God's power in Jesus' death on the cross is what I am going to call *the power of undefended love.*

The 'power in vulnerability' that we spoke about earlier need not imply the 'divesting of some clearly defined set of divine characteristics' that are shared with the Father,[15] nor is it merely the 'blueprint for a perfect human moral response', but a revelation of the 'humility of the divine nature'.[16] Jesus displays the self-giving humility which, we discover, is the essence of divinity. Divinity is humble rather than powerful, or as I want to describe it a power that comes from undefended love. This also means that we are most likely to see 'true divine empowerment'[17] in the context of vulnerability.

This doesn't mean that power no longer has any power, but that divine power is not the kind of power that we thought it was and which we would normally describe as powerful. Rather, it is an embodiment of the 'power . . . made perfect in weakness' that Paul speaks about (2 Corinthians 12:9). The message of the cross is indeed 'foolishness to those who are perishing, but to us who are being saved it is the power of God' (1 Corinthians 1:18).

This kind of power is most evident on the cross. The passion and death of Christ is the triumph of love. The power of the cross is not the power to overcome sin and evil by the exercise of greater strength or superior might, but the power of love to completely absorb and neutralise all that is thrown at it, even death itself. Christ forgives those who nail him to the cross.[18] He reaches out to those who are crucified alongside him.[19] He refuses to fight back. The crowds taunt him saying, 'He saved others; let him save himself if he is the

Messiah of God.'[20] Actually, he is saving everyone by losing himself. He is authentically walking the second mile of undefended love that he said should be the mark of his followers: denying themselves and taking up the cross each day.[21] The power to keep on loving when everyone else is full of wrath and hatred is the greatest power of all. It is the only way that hatred is defeated. It is the pattern of Christian discipleship.

When we conclude the Lord's Prayer by saying that power and glory belong to God, we are simply putting ourselves in right relationship with God as children of God's kingdom. We are acknowledging our dependence upon God and our gratitude for what God has done for us in Christ. We are clear about where our own affirmation comes from. We are sustained and upheld by the knowledge that we are known and loved. We know to whom we are accountable.

Christ is our saviour and our judge, our teacher and our friend. He leads us in ways that are undefended and vulnerable as one who is himself restful and contemplative, a person of prayer, shaped by the prayer he teaches us, recognising his need for rest and refreshment, one who knew himself to be the beloved. Thus in all prayer, and in the prayer we see in and receive from Jesus, we note what Coakley calls 'a special form of "vulnerability" which is not an invitation to be battered; nor is its silence a silencing . . . but by choosing to make a space in this way, one "practises the presence of God" – the subtle enabling presence of a God who neither shouts nor obliterates'.[22]

The invitation to abundant life

Jesus never used his power to impose his will upon anyone. The power of love is always an invitation (even if its compelling force feels like a summons). In all walks of life, we know love to be the greatest power of all. On the night before he died Jesus commanded his disciples to love one another and to love others in the same way that he had loved them.[23] This was how they would change the world. He not only said that there was no greater love than to lay down one's life for one's friends,[24] he showed them what this sort of love looked like.

It is the simplest thing in the world *not* to pray. Our lives and the life of our world are gravely imperilled by this. We cut ourselves off from the channels of grace and goodness that can change us. But many people don't pray, even those who are part of the Church. And the Lord's Prayer, though said often, is often said hurriedly and without reflection. Whereas, as we have been learning, we should tremble with awe at the beauty and majesty of these words, and what they mean for us. At the same time, they are simple to learn by heart. This is what we must do; and then commit to saying this prayer each day. And have our hearts changed.

Therefore, in a world where it is so easy and beguiling to look elsewhere, and where there are so many other seductive sources of glory and power and the rival claims of many kingdoms, we turn to Christ. We *acknowledge* that the kingdom, the power and the glory belong to God. We *see* the glory and the power of love that is shown to us in Christ as a revelation of God. We *receive and accept* the invitation to join in and be part of this kingdom. With Julian of Norwich, whose own profound reflections on the passion of Christ enabled her to write nearly seven hundred years ago, we too conclude: 'love was his meaning'.[25]

13.

AMEN

I wonder whether this apparently innocuous, even throw-away, word at the end of the Lord's Prayer – and, for that matter, at the end of every prayer – is actually the hardest one of all.

It means 'I agree'. We are therefore saying 'I agree' to some amazing, challenging and life-changing things. We are saying 'Amen' to each petition of the prayer as well as the whole prayer from top to bottom. In fact, in the old Visigothic liturgy of the Spanish church, this is exactly what happened. The priest would recite the Lord's Prayer petition by petition, and at the end of each one the people said 'Amen'.

Leonardo Boff, the great liberation theologian, said that 'being able to say Amen implies being able to trust and be confident and certain that everything is in the hands of the Father; for he has already conquered mistrust and fear, despite everything'.[1]

But do we have this trust?

The word means 'I give my assent'.

But do I give my assent?

It is said individually and corporately. I say 'Amen', but I say it *with* others. So it also means, as Stephen Cherry puts it, 'I agree – but also, so say all of us'.[2]

But do I agree?

Do I actually intend to do anything about this prayer? Am I, the rather presumptuous author of this book, ever actually intending to put into practice the things I write about and I'm expecting of you, the reader? As Michael Mayne expressed so honestly on the last page of his wonderful little book on prayer:

> My final concern is that you should be under no illusions about me: that you should understand that those who write books, or preach sermons, or give addresses on prayer, do so because of what they *lack*, not because of what they *have*. I have spoken of what I *long for*, not of what I possess; of how I would *like* to be, not of what I am. Of one who travels with you on the journey, sometimes tentatively, often not very confidently, yet always with hope, 'looking to Jesus, the author and perfector of our faith'.[3]

This is true for me too, as it may well be true for all of us. As it is true for so many other hundreds and thousands of Christian people who, though they still say 'Amen', know in their hearts that they haven't quite got there.

We agree with the prayer. We long to say 'Amen'. But we know that our lives are still far from alignment with the will of God; that the music of our lives is often discordant and obstructive of God's way.

So, first of all, just because I've written this book, please don't think that I know anything more about prayer than you do. And please don't think that my life is any better than yours. It most certainly isn't. Yet I see in this prayer my greatest hope. It is teaching me how to pray, and it is teaching me how to live.

I couldn't find the quotation I was looking for, but I remember reading somewhere that if you could say the Lord's Prayer once and truly mean it, then you would be in heaven. Well, if this is true then the fact that I'm still down here on earth plugging away at this prayer means I have not yet managed to say it and mean it. And this must be true for you, dear reader, as well.

However, I do not feel disheartened by this. I'm not beating myself up. First, because Jesus would never have taught us this prayer but for the fact we need it. And, second, I know I am in very good company, the company of Christian people down through the centuries who have said this prayer and tried to live by it. And I know that it will take a lifetime to learn to pray and live like Jesus. But that is exactly what God has given me. One lifetime.

So I take solace from Simone Weil, who wrote:

The Our Father contains all possible petitions . . . It is impossible to say at once through, giving the fullest possible attention to every word, without a change, infinitesimal perhaps, but real, taking place in the soul.[4]

And at a time in history where women and girls were afforded little opportunity for education or leadership and were often taught only the Hail Mary and the Lord's Prayer, as if they should be admitted to merely the foothills of the spiritual life, Teresa of Avila turned the tables on the so-called learned men, saying that if you say this prayer carefully you 'will soon find yourself reaching the summit of the mountain'.[5]

Or from the poet Edwin Muir, who wrote in his autobiography of his surprise and delight in unexpectedly finding himself doing just this:

Last night, going to bed alone, I suddenly found myself (I was taking off my waistcoat) reciting the Lord's Prayer in a loud emphatic voice – a thing I had not done for many years – with deep urgency and profound and disturbed emotions. While I went on I grew more composed; as if it had been empty and craving and were being replenished, my soul grew still; every word had a strange fullness of meaning which astonished and delighted me. It was late; I had sat up reading; I was sleepy; but as I stood in the middle of the floor half undressed saying the prayer over and over, meaning after meaning sprang from it; overcoming me again with joyful surprise; and I realised that simple petition was always universal and always inexhaustible, and day by day sanctified human life.[6]

And Henry Ward Beecher, who said:

I used to think the Lord's Prayer was a short prayer; but as I live longer, and see more of life, I begin to believe there is no such thing as getting through it. If someone, in praying that prayer, were to be stopped by every word until they had thoroughly prayed it, it would take a lifetime.[7]

Or Tom Wright, who said:

Learning to follow Jesus is simply learning to pray the Lord's Prayer.[8]

Or St Benedict, who because the Lord's Prayer was so important and so central said:

Definitely neither Lauds nor Vespers [two of the monastic offices that were said each day, what for us is now Morning and Evening Prayer] should finish without the Lord's Prayer being recited at the end by the superior, while all listen.[9]

Or from a colleague of mine, Ruth Richards, who when she heard I was writing this book told me that as a child she had a simple illustrated version of the Lord's Prayer, and it was this that taught her the faith and taught her to pray.

Or Pope Francis:

The prayer of Jesus, and therefore Christian prayer, is first a matter of making room for God, allowing him to manifest his Holiness in us, and also advancing his kingdom through the possibility of exercising his lordship of love in our lives.[10]

Or from Margaret Cundiff, who wrote:

The Lord's Prayer is a gift, the gift of Jesus to those who are serious about prayer. If my bookcases with all those helpful, beautiful, theological, philosophical views on prayer were to go up in flame tomorrow, if I was cast away on a desert island without even the guaranteed two books for every castaway on *Desert Island Discs* – the Bible and the complete works of Shakespeare – I would still have all I needed, the Lord's Prayer learned by heart.[11]

Or even Napoleon Bonaparte, who said this:

Do you wish to see that which is really sublime? Repeat the Lord's Prayer.[12]

SO WHAT IS PRAYER AND HOW DO I PRAY THE LORD'S PRAYER?

The real problem in prayer is not the absence of God but the absence of us. It's not that God isn't there; it's (nine times out of ten) that we're not. We are all over the place, entertaining memories, fantasies, anxieties. God is simply there in unending patience, saying to us, 'So when are you actually going to arrive? When are you going to sit and listen, to stop roaming about, and be present?'

ROWAN WILLIAMS[1]

The Lord's Prayer is the pattern and outline of all prayer. It gives us a language and a framework in which we can be present to God, praying with the very words of Jesus and therefore uniting our prayer with his prayer. As Robert Warren puts it, the Lord's Prayer teaches us 'how to pray . . . it embodies Jesus' whole teaching in a few memorable phrases . . . and it gives expression to the way of life that should arise out of such teaching'.[2]

Jesus gave his disciples this simple prayer for them to memorise. He did not exhort them to spend hours in meditation, nor did he expect them always to be able to express prayer in their own words. Of course he longed for them to grow into the same intimate relationship with God that we see exemplified in his ministry, but Jesus' first priority was to give them a prayer that would be the foundation and the heart of all prayer.

We've always known this. That's why teaching and learning the Lord's Prayer was so central to initiation and formation in the Christian faith in the first centuries of the Church's life. And has been ever since. Writing to Bishop Ecgbert in 734, the Venerable Bede, one of the great saints of the north and one of the foremost biblical scholars of his day and the first historian of the English church, gently chastised the bishop for not paying enough attention to this bit of his ministry.

'Above all else,' he wrote,

you must endeavour with all diligence to see that the catholic faith which is contained in the Apostles' Creed and the Lord's Prayer . . . be rooted deeply in the memory of all which belong unto your rule: It is true that these things have become perfectly known to those who have been taught to read the Latin tongue; but do you cause them to be known and constantly repeated in their own tongue by those who are unlearned, that is, by them who have knowledge only of their proper tongue . . . By this means it cometh to pass that the whole body of believers shall learn how they should believe, and fortify and arm themselves by steadfast belief . . . By this means it cometh that the whole band of them that worship God shall understand what most they are bound to seek of the Divine Mercy. For the which reason I have myself too ofttimes given to unlearned priests both these things, to wit, the Creed and the Lord's Prayer translated into the English tongue.[3]

Part of my great hope for this book is that I, and those who work with me, may do in our day what Bede did in his: teach people the Lord's Prayer.[4]

Many centuries ago, Cyprian noted that Jesus didn't only give us 'the form by which to pray, and himself guided and directed the purpose of our prayer . . . he taught us not by words alone, but by deeds . . . He himself prayed frequently, pleading and showing us by the testimony of his example.'[5]

We therefore learn to pray by using the words Jesus gave us. Or put it another way: we learn to pray *by praying*. We do it. We begin (which is always the hardest part of anything). We learn from Jesus. We learn to pray by heart.

We follow Jesus' example. We set aside times for prayer. We nurture that desire for God that we see so clearly in his life and ministry. We adopt the disciplines that will be necessary for a prayerful life, because we know that desire won't always be available.

Paul says, 'pray without ceasing' (1 Thessalonians 5:17). I don't think he means that we should do the activity we call prayer all the time, but rather make our lives a prayer. Make your life a hymn of praise to God, so that your life speaks of the things of God and the beauty of God, and people might even see and hear Christ in you.

This can only happen when prayer gets to the heart of us. And it will be the simple disciplines and the daily repetition of the Lord's Prayer that will help the most.

Prayer is relationship with God for others

Prayer is relationship with God. That's what the Lord's Prayer teaches us first of all. 'He is our Father,' said Pope Francis. 'I am not an only child.'[6] As we have been exploring throughout this book, prayer is also relationship with others – we pray together – and it is relationship with God *for* others and *for* the world. It creates relationship *with* God and *with* others. It carries responsibility. It is relationship *with* God *for* others.

Spoken from the heart of God through the heart of Jesus to the heart of the world – and through the hearts of all those who have learned it by heart, that is through *us*, the Lord's Prayer teaches us to pray and teaches us to live.

When we don't know what to pray – but also when we do! – we turn to this prayer because this prayer says everything. Praying these words by heart, we learn to live as God intended us to live, to live like Jesus.

If we have a teaching or preaching ministry in the Church, we need to take Bede's words to heart. Are we teaching people the Lord's Prayer? And are we teaching people what it means?

As it is just about the only prayer that is still well known in our wider culture, we need to take every opportunity to say it, probably using the traditional version, since this is the one that is still known by those outside the Church. But we also need to recognise that many people today don't know it. It is our responsibility to do something about this. Therefore, let us make the most of every opportunity to teach people the Lord's Prayer and to teach people about the Lord's Prayer. Our culture is in danger of losing a precious gift, a way of praying and a compass for life, without it.

We need to set a good example, saying it every day; letting it dwell in us and shape who we are and how we live.

This is what prayer does. It changes us, because by the Holy Spirit God is praying in us. This is most apparent when we use the very words Jesus gave us.

In church, where the Lord's Prayer is always part of the set pattern of worship, it is sometimes introduced by the words, 'As our Saviour taught us, we are bold to say. . .' Or in *Common Worship*, the set prayers for the Church of England, the priest is instructed to say as the Lord's Prayer is introduced, 'Let us pray with confidence as our Saviour has taught us . . .'[7] This boldness, this confidence, is what we need. A boldness and a confidence to put the Lord's Prayer, and to put the discipline and joy of prayer and the challenging and beautiful ideas this prayer speaks about, at the centre of life. And of course, when we come forward to receive Holy Communion, praying for our daily bread, what we hope to receive takes on a special relevance. This is why from a very early point in the development of the Church's liturgy, the Lord's Prayer started to be said just before we receive Communion.

A manifesto for the heart: How should I say the Lord's Prayer?

Slowly.
Regularly.
Carefully.
Intentionally.
Expectantly.
Humbly.

Self-forgetfully.
Joyfully.
On your own.
With others.
Doing the washing up.
In the shower.
On the train.
Stuck in the traffic jam on the way to work.
In the queue at the checkout.
At the top of mountains.
Before receiving Holy Communion.
Sitting down afterwards.
In times of great sorrow.
In times of great joy.
When a child is born.
When vows are exchanged.
When you don't have any other words to say.
When you are frightened or lonely.
When you feel like giving up.
Holding the hands of your loved ones when they die.

We say the Lord's Prayer each day. It should be at the centre of our devotional life. We should savour and weigh each petition carefully. Its boldness speaks of the very challenging nature of what it commits us to. We are to love God; to love each other; to seek God's will and work for God's kingdom; to want only that which is sufficient and enough; to share our bread with others; to be penitent and ready to forgive; and to know and pray that, throughout all this, God will be with us in trial and temptation, and that all power and glory belong to God.

Which is why, even on our death bed, or we might say

especially on our death bed, this prayer is there for us. It is inside us and it will have become part of us.

But until that day, and because it is the one prayer we will definitely know by heart, we can say it anywhere and everywhere.

Jesus has given us a manifesto for the heart, a way of praying and a way of enjoying communion with God.

It is one of the ways Jesus is always with us: his words and his very presence dwelling in our hearts and uttered by our lips, uniting our hearts and our voices to his heart and his voice, and leading us on the way that is to life.

READING, STUDYING AND PRAYING THIS BOOK WITH OTHERS

Praying by Heart: The Lord's Prayer for everyone takes us through the Lord's Prayer line by line.

Obviously, you can read it on your own or, having read it, share it with someone else and then discuss with them what you both made of it. But if you want to use this book in a more formal Lent or Advent study group, a reading group or any other church study group you may find that the four sections give you some shape and pattern, though as you will see, Parts 2 and 3 are much longer than the others and there is quite a lot of material to cover. However, I think there may be some benefit from approaching the book in this way, beginning with the 'Getting Started' chapter and then looking at a different part each week.

So, each week everyone reads the relevant section in the book. When they come to the session, they are asked to share what they made of it and what questions emerge for them. Discussing these questions may be more than enough to fill the time, and it is always good to be led by the questions people actually have rather than the ones provided in the book. But each week you can also pose some or all of the following specific questions:

Week 1: Getting started

Questions:
- When did you first learn the Lord's Prayer and from whom?
- What excites you about it?
- What puzzles you?
- What challenges you?
- Do you have a view as to whether we should use the word 'sin' or 'trespass'?

Week 2: Our Father

Questions:
- What does it mean for you to think of God as Father?
- Do you have a view as to whether we should also call God 'Mother'?
- What does it mean for you to think of God as *our* Father?
- How do you think we should express our responsibilities to one another as sisters and brothers in Christ?
- Have you had any experiences where knowing God as Father and knowing God as *our* Father have changed the way you behave or act?

Week 3: Hallowed be your name, your kingdom come, your will be done on earth as in heaven

Questions:
- What language do you find the most helpful to use when you speak to God?
- How easy do you find it to give voice to your needs and hopes before God?
- How does this prayer change them?
- How would you describe the kingdom of God to someone who has never been to church or read the Bible?
- What do you find hardest and most challenging about praying 'God's will be done'?
- How would you describe a world where heaven fills earth? (Perhaps express this last question in a poem or a prayer that can then be shared with others.)

Week 4: Give us today our daily bread, forgive us our sins, as we forgive those who sin against us, and lead us not into temptation, but deliver us from evil

Questions:
- What in your view does 'enough' look like?
- What changes would you expect to see in the world and in your own life if we lived with just enough?
- We know we need to be forgiven ourselves, but should we always forgive others? Are there exceptions?
- Do you have any experience of being forgiven or of forgiving others that has helped you understand the nature of forgiveness?

Week 5: For the kingdom, the power and the glory are yours now and for ever. Amen

Questions:
- Which bit of the Lord's Prayer do you find it easiest to say 'Amen' to?
- And which bits are the hardest?
- Do you have any experience of where prayer, and especially the Lord's Prayer, has changed you or someone you know?
- As we finish reading the book, which bits of the book have challenged you the most?
- Which have given you the greatest joy and the greatest hope?
- What are you now going to do to ensure that the Lord's Prayer is a part of your daily prayer and how might you share this with others?

Perhaps finish your time together by everyone writing their top tips for prayer and sharing them with each other. Or you could even write your own versions of the Lord's Prayer and discuss them together.

Notes for leaders

Each session should begin with some refreshments. Welcome people and read the Lord's Prayer from Scripture, either the version in Matthew, reading from Matthew 6:5–14, or the one from Luke 11:1–4 (both these passages are given below). Note how they both speak about *when* we pray. Then, based on your own reading and understanding, briefly introduce the section to be studied in the session. After the questions and discussion, lead everyone in a slow, prayerful reading of the Lord's Prayer and any other prayers that seem appropriate.

Matthew 6:5–15 (NRSV)

[Jesus said] 'And whenever you pray, do not be like the hypocrites; for they love to stand and pray in the synagogues and at the street corners, so that they may be seen by others. Truly I tell you, they have received their reward. But whenever you pray, go into your room and shut the door and pray to your Father who is in secret; and your Father who sees in secret will reward you.

'When you are praying, do not heap up empty phrases as the Gentiles do; for they think that they will be heard because of their many words. Do not be like them, for your Father knows what you need before you ask him.

'Pray then in this way:

> *Our Father in heaven,*
> *hallowed be your name.*
> *Your kingdom come.*
> *Your will be done,*
>   *on earth as it is in heaven.*
> *Give us this day our daily bread.*
> *And forgive us our debts,*
>   *as we also have forgiven our debtors.*
> *And do not bring us to the time of trial,*
>   *but rescue us from the evil one.*

For if you forgive others their trespasses, your heavenly Father will also forgive you; but if you do not forgive others, neither will your Father forgive your trespasses.'

Luke 11:1–4

[Jesus] was praying in a certain place, and after he had finished, one of his disciples said to him, 'Lord, teach us to pray, as John taught his disciples.' He said to them, 'When you pray, say:

> *Father, hallowed be your name.*
> *Your kingdom come.*
> *Give us each day our daily bread.*
> *And forgive us our sins,*
> *for we ourselves forgive everyone*
> *indebted to us.*
> *And do not bring us to the time of*
> *trial.'*

When we come to the Lord's Prayer, we are coming home.

KENNETH STEVENSON[1]

ACKNOWLEDGEMENTS

I don't know for sure who taught me the Lord's Prayer. It was almost certainly my parents, but it would have been reinforced at school and then, when I started going to church, my understanding of the prayer would have been unpacked, deepened and developed by many sermons, Bible studies and study groups. I also remember during my formation for ordained ministry writing a long essay on the place of the Lord's Prayer in the liturgy of the early church. Therefore, all that I've written in this book has been shaped by many other influences and many other voices.

In the work I'm currently doing for the Church of England across the province of York, teaching about the Lord's Prayer is part of an initiative called *Faith in the North*. You can find out more about this here: https://www.archbishopofyork.org/faith-in-the-north. In the coming years I hope to teach the Lord's Prayer to everyone in the north. The book itself, and its emphasis on the prayer as a pattern for life as well as a pattern for prayer, is influenced by this calling. In particular my colleagues Elizabeth Addy, Mark Powley and Mark Steadman have read through earlier drafts of the book and contributed all sorts of helpful and insightful comments. I owe them a debt of gratitude. Any mistakes or shortcomings in the book, however, are entirely my own.

Finally, I am also very grateful to my PA, Alison Cundiff, for her organisation of my diary which has helped me carve out time to write, and to the team at Hodder for their encouragement and support for the book and all I hope it might achieve. In particular, Joanna Davey read the text very closely. Her comments have improved the book, giving it much greater clarity.

Jesus taught his disciples to pray. His words become ours. I hope that this little book will lead you into understanding these words more clearly and letting this prayer shape your life as it has shaped mine.

Bishopthorpe
Eastertide 2024

NOTES

Epigraph

1 Thérèse of Lisieux, *Autobiography of a Saint*, trans. Ronald Knox (Fount, 1958), p. 229.
2 Tom Wright, *God and the Pandemic: A Christian Reflection on the Coronavirus and its Aftermath* (SPCK, 2020), p. 19.

Preface

1 See Luke 11:1.
2 John Dominic Crossan, *The Greatest Prayer: Rediscovering the Revolutionary Message of the Lord's Prayer* (SPCK, 2010), p. 182.

1. Getting Started

1 Teresa of Avila, *The Way of Perfection*, trans. E. Peters (Sheed & Ward, 1999), p. 89.
2 Tom Wright, *The Lord and His Prayer* (SPCK, 1996), p. 2.
3 Robert Warren, *An Affair of the Heart: How to Pray More Effectively* (Highland Books, 1994), p. 157.
4 Austin Farrer, *Words for Life: Forty Meditations – Previously Unpublished*, ed. Charles Conti and Leslie Houlden (SPCK, 2012), p. 1.

Notes

Part 1: Our Father in heaven

1 Pope Francis, *The Lord's Prayer*, address given in the New Orthodox Cathedral in Bucharest as part of his Apostolic Journey to Romania, 31 May 2019, p. 1.
2 Pope Francis, *Our Father: Reflections on the Lord's Prayer* (Rider, 2017), pp. 11–12.

2. Father – the intimacy and affirmation of love

1 Donald Coggan, *The Prayers of the New Testament* (Hodder & Stoughton, 1967), p. 19. Donald Coggan wrote this book while he was Archbishop of York and at Bishopthorpe where I now live. I note it was also published by the same publisher as this one!
2 'A Song of Anselm' in *Common Worship: Daily Prayer* (Church House Publishing, 2005), p. 639.
3 Julian of Norwich, *Revelations of Divine Love*, trans. and with an introduction by Clifton Wolters (Penguin Books, 1966), p. 167.
4 Julian of Norwich, *Revelations of Divine Love*, p. 167.
5 Julian of Norwich, *Revelations of Divine Love*, p. 170.
6 Julian of Norwich, *Revelations of Divine Love*, p. 171.
7 Stephen Cherry, *Thy Will Be Done* (Bloomsbury Continuum, 2020), p. 15.
8 See Romans 8:35–39.
9 See Luke 15:7.
10 See Matthew 18:4.

3. Our – the beautiful challenge of belonging

1 Pope Francis, *Our Father: Reflections on the Lord's Prayer* (Rider, 2017), p. 13.
2 Hugh Latimer, 'First Sermon on the Lord's Prayer', in *The Works of Hugh Latimer*, ed. G. E. Corrie (Cambridge: Parker Society, 1844), p. 338; from *Love's Redeeming Work: The Anglican Quest for Holiness*, compiled by Geoffrey Rowell, Kenneth Stevenson and Rowan Williams (Oxford University Press, 2002), p. 17.

Part 2: Three hearty praises

1 Michael Mayne, *Prayer* (Darton, Longman & Todd, 2013), p. 48.

2 John Dominic Crossan, *The Greatest Prayer: Rediscovering the Revolutionary Message of the Lord's Prayer* (SPCK, 2010), p. 47.

3 John Dominic Crossan, *The Greatest Prayer,* p. 57.

4 Robert Warren, *An Affair of the Heart: How to Pray More Effectively* (Highland Books, 1994), p. 150.

4. Hallowed be your name

1 Tom Wright, *The Lord and His Prayer* (SPCK, 1996), p. 7.

2 Hans Urs von Balthasar, *Glory of the Lord, Theological Aesthetics: Volume II* (Ignatius Press, 2012), p. 206.

3 Hans Urs von Balthasar, *Glory of the Lord,* p. 168.

4 Stephen Cherry, *Thy Will Be Done* (Bloomsbury Continuum, 2020), p. 36.

5 I borrow here an arresting phrase of Stephen Cherry's. Stephen Cherry, *Thy Will Be Done,* p. 36.

6 See Stephen Cottrell, *Dear England: Finding Hope, Taking Heart and Changing the World* (Hodder & Stoughton, 2021), pp. 143 –5.

7 Evelyn Underhill, quoted in Robyn Wrigley Carr, *Music of Eternity: Meditations for Advent with Evelyn Underhill* (SPCK, 2021), p. 29.

8 Robyn Wrigley Carr, *Music of Eternity,* p. 30.

9 See Exodus 3:5.

10 Tom Wright, *The Lord and His Prayer,* p. 12.

5. Your kingdom come

1 Kingly titles are used for Jesus in Revelation 19, but Jesus certainly never claims to be a king like Caesar, and in his new creation all people reign (Revelation 22:5).

2 Robert Warren, *Living Well* (HarperCollins, 1998).

3 Robert Warren, *Living Well.*

4 I am grateful to Mark Powley for pointing me towards these connections and their difference and to C. Wess Daniels, Gathering In Light +

Qaddish and The Lord's Prayer: Jesus' Subversive Tactics, accessed 7 January 2024.

6. Your will be done

1 See John 14:2–3. These two verses sum up the whole Christian hope. Through his death and resurrection Jesus prepares a place for us in glory, so that we will be in him and with him for eternity. It is a passage often read at funeral services.
2 Stephen Cherry, *Thy Will Be Done* (Bloomsbury Continuum, 2020), p. 207.

7. On earth as in heaven

1 Mark Powley: one of his comments in the margin of the text after he had read through a first draft of the book.
2 Tom Wright, *God and the Pandemic: A Christian Reflection on the Coronavirus and its Aftermath* (SPCK, 2020), p. 34.
3 This little phrase comes from a poem I have written about prayer called 'Unconfounded'. It is not yet published. It imagines one person listening to another person praying and in so doing learning what prayer is, and especially learning about desire. As you read the poem you might wonder whether the person being listened to is Christ.

Part 3: Three humble requests

1 Kenneth Stevenson, *Abba Father: Understanding and Using the Lord's Prayer* (Canterbury Press, 2000), p. 34.
2 Pope Francis, *Our Father: Reflections on the Lord's Prayer* (Rider, 2017), p. 46.
3 Jeremy Taylor, in Reginald Heber (ed.), *The Whole Works of Jeremy Taylor: Vol III* (Rivingtons, 1888), p. 79, quoted in Kenneth Stevenson, *Abba Father: Understanding and Using the Lord's Prayer*, p. 40.
4 John Dominic Crossan, *The Greatest Prayer: Rediscovering the Revolutionary Message of the Lord's Prayer* (SPCK, 2010), p. 48.

8. Give us today our daily bread

1   https://www.theguardian.com/news/2019/dec/05/gap-between-rich-and-poor-grows-alongside-rise-in-uks-total-wealth. Accessed 16 June 2020.

2   https://www.childrenssociety.org.uk/what-we-do/our-work/ending-child-poverty. The measure for poverty used is a child living in a family whose income is below 60 per cent of the UK's average after adjusting for family size. Even if you disagree with this measure, you are still left with a shockingly inequitable distribution of income and opportunity. It means, for instance, that there are couples in the UK living with two children and having less than £58 per day to live on: that's slightly less than £15 per person. So, after housing costs, which for such a family would usually be paid by other benefits, there is £15 per person per day for food, clothes, bills, transport and childcare if needed, let alone school trips and other activities wealthier families take for granted. Accessed 16 June 2020.

3   Pope Francis, *Let Us Dream: The Path to a Better Future* (Simon & Schuster, 2020), p. 44.

4   Pope Francis, *Our Father: Reflections on the Lord's Prayer* (Rider, 2017), p. 110.

5   Michael J. Sandal, *What Money Can't Buy: The Moral Limits of Markets* (Penguin Books, 2013), p. 10.

6   I am indebted to John Dominic Crossan who makes this point in his book *The Greatest Prayer: Rediscovering the Revolutionary Message of the Lord's Prayer* (HarperCollins, 2010), p. 40.

7   Jonathan Porritt, *Capitalism as if the World Matters* (Earthscape, 2005), p. 324.

8   Sandal, *What Money Can't Buy*, p. 112.

9   There is a good discussion of this in Kenneth Stevenson, *Abba Father: Understanding and Using the Lord's Prayer* (Canterbury Press, 2000), pp. 93–4.

10 Kenneth Stevenson, *Abba Father: Understanding and Using the Lord's Prayer*, p. 94.

11 Crossan, *The Greatest Prayer*, p. 138.

12 Pope Francis, *Our Father: Reflections on the Lord's Prayer*, p. 78.

13 Pope Francis, *Our Father: Reflections on the Lord's Prayer*, p. 74.

14 Mark Powley, *Consumer Detox* (Zondervan, 2010), p. 83.

9. Forgive us our sins

1 Augustine, *Sermon 56.12*; see Edmond Hill (trans.), *The Works of St Augustine: Sermons III* (New City Press, 1999), p. 97.

10. As we forgive those who sin against us

1 Stephen Cherry, *Thy Will Be Done* (Bloomsbury Continuum, 2020), p. 140.
2 Mark Powley: another note written in the margin of the first draft of this book.
3 Quoted in Adrian Hastings, *A History of English Christianity, 1920 –1985* (Collins, 1986), pp. 385–6.

11. Lead us not into temptation, but deliver us from evil

1 Stephen Cherry, *Thy Will Be Done* (Bloomsbury Continuum, 2020), p. 152.
2 See Stephen Cottrell, *The Things He Said* (SPCK, 2009).
3 *The Book of Common Prayer: The Texts of 1549, 1559, and 1662*, ed. with an introduction and notes by Brian Cummings (Oxford University Press, 2011), p. 254.
4 Tom Wright, *The Lord and His Prayer* (SPCK, 1996), p. 72.
5 John Dominic Crossan, *The Greatest Prayer: Rediscovering the Revolutionary Message of the Lord's Prayer* (SPCK, 2010), p. 185.

Part 4: For the kingdom, the power and the glory are yours, now and for ever

1 Origen, 'On Prayer', in *Tertullian, Cyprian and Origen on the Lord's Prayer*, trans. Alistair Stewart-Sykes (St Vladimir's Seminary Press, 2004), p. 213.

12. Kingdom, power and glory for ever

1 These so-called *sources of power* were first categorised in 1959 by psychologists John French and Bertram Raven. See J. R. P. French and B. Raven, 'The bases of social power' in D. Cartwright (ed.), *Studies in Social Power* (Ann Arbor, MI: University of Michigan Press, 1959). Building on this seminal work, Roy Oswald applied this thinking to the Church. See *Power Analysis of a Congregation* (Alban Institute, 1981). Using Oswald's categories, Roger Matthews very helpfully defines seven types of power in a way that can encourage leaders to identify where their power lies and how power is distributed and exercised by different individuals in different contexts. Roger Matthews, *A leadership workshop for the Diocesan Bishops of Embu, Kirinyaga, Marsabit, Mbere and Meru, 18–21 October 2016, Keep Watch Over Yourself, Take Care of the Flock (Acts 20.28) Leading Ourselves, Leading Others, Being Led and Leading the Way*, p. 27.

2 John Kotter, *Power and Influence* (Free Press, 1985), p. 86.

3 David M. Gitari, *Responsible Church Leadership* (Action Publishers, 2005), pp. 137–8.

4 David M. Gitari, *Responsible Church Leadership*, p. 139.

5 See John 14:9.

6 Sarah Coakley, *Powers and Submissions: Spirituality, Philosophy and Gender* (Blackwell Publishing, 2002), p. 5.

7 Jesus is silent before the high priest (Matthew 26:57–63). He refuses to answer Pilate (John 19:9). Interestingly, the discussion they do have is about the nature and source of power.

8 After Christ's arrest in Gethsemane, Mark tells us that 'all of them deserted him and fled' (Mark 14:50).

9 Matthew 8:27.

10 On the cross Christ is derided by onlookers (Mark 15:29–30), by the scribes and chief priests (Mark 15:31–32), and even mocked by those who are crucified alongside him (Luke 23:39) but he does not act, rather allowing himself to be acted upon.

11 Eduard Schweizer, *The Good News According to Matthew* (SPCK, 1976), p. 193 (and unlike the version in Mark, where this is just said of Jesus as a self-evident fact: see Mark 1:22).

12 Matthew 5:41.

13 Matthew 5:44.

14 'Why else did a woman who had lived a sinful life dare to burst into a dinner party of religious leaders to break a jar of expensive perfume over his feet (Luke 7:37–50)? Why did a blind man cry out over the dismissive crowd, "Jesus, Son of David, have mercy on me" (Luke 18. 36–43)? Because they both saw in [Jesus] someone they could trust.' James Lawrence, *Growing Leaders, Reflections on Leadership, Life and Jesus* (Bible Reading Fellowship, 2004), p. 180.

15 Sarah Coakley, *Powers and Submissions*, p. 9.

16 Sarah Coakley, *Powers and Submissions*, p. 10.

17 Sarah Coakley, *Powers and Submissions*, p. 32.

18 Luke 23:34.

19 Luke 23:43.

20 Luke 23:35.

21 Luke 9:23.

22 Coakley, *Powers and Submissions*, p. 35.

23 John 15:12.

24 John 15:13.

25 Julian of Norwich, *Revelations of Divine Love*, trans. with an introduction by Clifton Wolters (Penguin Books, 1966), p. 211.

13. Amen

1 Leonardo Boff, *The Lord's Prayer: The Prayer of Integral Liberation* (Orbis, 1983), p. 122.

2 Stephen Cherry, *Thy Will Be Done* (Bloomsbury Continuum, 2020), p. 200.

3 Michael Mayne, *Prayer* (Darton, Longman & Todd, 2013), p. 62.

4 Simone Weil, quoted in Michael Mayne, *Prayer*, p. 56.

5 Teresa of Avila, *The Way of Perfection*, trans. E. Allison Peters (Sheed & Ward, 1999), p. 68.

6 Edwin Muir, *An Autobiography* (Methuen, 1964), p. 246. This beautiful and powerful quotation is in Michael Mayne, *Prayer*, p. 56 and in Kenneth Stevenson, *Abba Father: Understanding and Using the Lord's Prayer* (Canterbury Press, 2000), p. 21.

7 Henry Ward Beecher, https://livinghour.org/lords-prayer/quotes/. Accessed 27 October 2023.

8 Tom Wright, *God and the Pandemic: A Christian Reflection on the Coronavirus and its Aftermath* (SPCK, 2020), p. 19.

9 *The Rule of St Benedict*, trans. Abbot Parry OSB with an introduction and commentary by Esther de Waal (Gracewing, 1990), p. 35.

10 Pope Francis, *Our Father: Reflections on the Lord's Prayer* (Rider, 2017), p. 46.

11 Margaret Cundiff, *Living by the Book: A Personal Journey through the Sermon on the Mount* (Bible Reading Fellowship, 1999), p. 71.

12 Napoleon Bonaparte, https://livinghour.org/lords-prayer/quotes/. Accessed 27 October 2023.

Epilogue

1 Rowan Williams, *Being Disciples: Essentials of the Christian Life* (SPCK, 2016), p. 81.

2 Robert Warren, *An Affair of the Heart: How to Pray More Effectively* (Highland Books, 1994), p. 157.

3 Bede, *Letter to Bishop Ecgbert* and shared with me by my colleague Dee Dyas, to whom I am greatly indebted.

4 This initiative to teach the Lord's Prayer is being promoted across the north under the heading *Faith in the North*.

5 Cyprian, 'On the Lord's Prayer' in 'On Prayer' in *Tertullian, Cyprian and Origen on the Lord's Prayer*, trans. Alistair Stewart-Sykes (St Vladimir's Seminary Press, 2004), pp. 65, 86.

6 Pope Francis, *Our Father: Reflections on the Lord's Prayer* (Rider, 2017), p. 13.

7 *The Order for the Celebration of Holy Communion, Order One, Services and Prayers for the Church of England* (Church House Publishing, 2000), p. 178.

Epigraph

1 Kenneth Stevenson, *Abba Father: Understanding and Using the Lord's Prayer* (Canterbury Press, 2000), p. 54.

HODDER &
STOUGHTON

Hodder & Stoughton is the UK's
leading Christian publisher,
with a wide range of books from
the bestselling authors in the UK
and around the world ranging from
Christian lifestyle and theology to
apologetics, testimony and fiction.
We also publish the world's
most popular Bible translation
in modern English, the New
International Version, renowned
for its accuracy and readability.

Hodderfaith.com   Hodderbibles.co.uk
@HodderFaith   /HodderFaith